Sweet Surprises

Some Light, M
All Delicio...

Compiled By
Professional Home Economics Teachers
of California, Nevada, and Arizona

Editor
Gerry Murry Henderson

Graphic Design, Typography and Production
Younge West Advertising, Fullerton, CA

Library of Congress Catalog
Card No. 83-072752
ISBN 0-914159-14-3

Sweet Surprises

(How It "Comes Together")

The HOME ECONOMICS TEACHERS of California, Arizona, and Nevada, who contributed all the recipes in this book, are the "heart and soul" of all California Cookbook Publications. Not only are these TEACHERS dedicated to preparing the youth of our Nation for their "careers in technology", they also contribute their BEST RECIPES to these books each year! GERRY MURRY HENDERSON teaches full time at Temple City High School, and also finds time to carefully EDIT our books each year. NANCY FREEMAN, our office manager, receives and "processes" each and every recipe on the computer, along with managing all CCC business. DOUG HERREMA, on staff for 17 years, carefully selects Publications Titles each year and is responsible for all foods photos. DOUG PIERCE, also on staff for 17 years, travels further, collects more recipes, and usually outsells all of us! Certain people "never grow old" and continue to be our "pony express" at CCC: RUSS HERREMA, who showed us all "how to run a business"; BILL HORTON, who was never "too busy" to help; BILL O'BRIEN, who "saved us" in Northern California; and BILL (RICH) RICHARDSON, with an engineering background, who works so efficiently, and helps me figure out "the cost of everything"! THANKS GUYS - can't "do it" without you!

And certain foods companies have made possible all the foods photography in this book: Dole Foods, San Francisco, CA; General Mills of Minneapolis, MN; Hershey Foods of Hershey, PA; Pillsbury Company of Minneapolis, MN.

And I, as the owner, am the lucky guy who gets to work with "all of the above"! THANK YOU, for your purchase of this book!

Sincerely,

Grady W. Reed

Grady W. Reed, Owner
California Cookbook Company

P.S. PLEASE NOTE REORDER FORM ON PAGE 160!

TABLE OF CONTENTS:

On our Front Cover:
Brownie Macaroon Torte, p. 7
Courtesy of Pillsbury Co. Minn. MN

Professional Home Economics Teachers
Advisory Committee

Amy Bean
Cabrillo High School, Lompoc

Mary Carr
Enterprise High School, Redding

Simone Clements
Bret Harte High School, Angels Camp

Carole Delap
Golden West High School, Visalia

Cindy Elledge
Hohansen High School, Modesto

Pam Fecchino
Cimmaron-Memorial High School
Las Vegas, Nevada

Pam Ford
Temecula Valley High School, Temecula

Donna Hamilton
Del Oro High School, Loomis

Gerry Henderson
Temple City High School, Temple City

Gage Hewes
So. Pasadena High School, So. Pasadena

Grace Hibma
Office of L.A. County Superintendent of
Schools, Consultant Consumer
& Homemaking Education

Donna Hulen, Career Consultants
Los Alamitos High School, Los Alamitos

Dottie Jones
Etiwanda High School, Etiwanda

Mary Lash
Paramount High School, Paramount

Helen Lievre
La Cañada High School, La Cañada

Karen Lopez
San Luis Obispo High School,
San Luis Obispo

Jeri Lundy
Grossmont High School, La Mesa

Darlene Lupul
Tokay High School, Lodi

Dale Matsuno
Bell Gardens High School, Bell Gardens

Doris Oitzman
Victor Valley High School, Victorville

Linda Paskins
Cordova High School, Rancho Cordova

Susie Pendleton
Cerritos High School, Cerritos

Roberta Priestley
Alhambra High School, Alhambra

Mary Rector
Valley High School, Las Vegas, Nevada

April Rosenthal
Chino High School, Chino

Lynda Ruth
La Mirada High School, La Mirada

Marianne Traw
Ball Junior High School, Anaheim

Sonja Tyree
Ayala High School, Chino Hills

Sue Walters
Morse High School, San Diego

Betty Wells
Bidwell Junior High School, Chico

Kathryn P. Whitten
Regional Supervisor Home Economics
Education, Fresno

4

Cakes and Frostings

Almond Sherry Cake

Serves 10 - 12

Streusel Filling:
⅓ cup brown sugar, firmly packed
¼ cup flour
3 tablespoons butter, firm
½ teaspoon cinnamon
¾ cup almonds, toasted, sliced

Sherry Cake:
1 (18.5 ounce) package yellow cake mix (without pudding)
4 large eggs
¾ cup cream sherry
¾ cup vegetable oil
1 (3.75 ounce) package instant vanilla pudding
½ teaspoon nutmeg

Sherry Glaze:
2 cups powdered sugar, sifted
⅓ cup butter, melted
1 tablespoon cream sherry
1 to 2 teaspoons hot water
Garnish: ¼ cup almonds, toasted, sliced

Preheat oven to 350 degrees. Streusel filling: Combine brown sugar, flour, butter and cinnamon until crumbly. Stir in almonds; set aside. Cake: Combine cake mix, eggs, sherry, oil, pudding mix and nutmeg. Mix at low speed 1 minute; scraping bowl constantly. Mix at medium speed 3 minutes, scraping bowl occasionally, or by hand 5 minutes. Pour half of the batter into a greased and floured 10" bundt pan. Sprinkle streusel filling evenly over batter in pan. Pour in remaining cake batter. Bake 45 to 50 minutes, or until cake springs back when lightly touched in center. Cool on wire rack 15 minutes. Unmold from pan; cool completely on rack. Sherry Glaze: Combine powdered sugar, melted butter and sherry. Stir in enough hot water to make a glaze of desired consistency. Glaze top of cake and garnish with almonds, if desired.

"This "easy to make" cake is a recipe from a Blue Diamond Almond Cookbook I have."

Jan Neufeld   **Fullerton High School, Fullerton, CA**

Apple Hill Cake

Serves 12

2 eggs
2 cups sugar
½ cup oil
1 teaspoon vanilla
2 cups flour
2 teaspoons baking soda
2 teaspoons cinnamon
1 teaspoon nutmeg
¼ teaspoon salt
4 cups apples, finely diced
1 cup nuts, chopped

Preheat oven to 350 degrees. In large mixing bowl, beat eggs well. Add sugar and beat again. Beat in oil and vanilla. In separate bowl, sift together flour, baking soda, cinnamon, nutmeg and salt. Add to creamed mixture. Stir in apples and nuts and pour into a greased and floured 13" x 9" x 2" pan. Bake 45 to 55 minutes. Cake should be very, very moist.

"Handed down from my mother, Yvonne Jones."

Anne Cornell   **Turlock High School, Turlock, CA**

Banana Pound Cake

Makes 2 loaves

1 package yellow cake mix
4 eggs
⅓ cup oil
½ cup water
4 very ripe bananas, mashed
1 small box instant banana pudding
1 ½ teaspoons cinnamon
½ teaspoon nutmeg

Preheat oven to 350 degrees. Combine all ingredients and mix well. Pour into 2 lightly greased loaf pans. Bake 1 hour, or until knife inserted in center comes out clean.

"This pound cake is great by itself - my boys love cream cheese frosting on top."

LaRae Harguess   **Hesperia High School, Hesperia, CA**

Banana Split Cake

Serves 12

2 packages graham crackers, crushed
1 cup margarine, divided and softened
1 (8 ounce) package cream cheese
1 pound powdered sugar
1 teaspoon vanilla
1 (20 ounce) can crushed pineapple, drained
2 large bananas
1 (12 ounce) container Cool Whip
Garnish: maraschino cherries, ½ cup chopped nuts

Crush graham crackers and mix with ½ cup margarine. Spread in bottom of 13" x 9" pan. Cream the cheese, sugar, vanilla and remaining ½ cup margarine until fluffy. Layer this on top of graham crackers. Spread with partially drained pineapple; top with sliced banana and spread Cool Whip on top. Garnish as desired with cherries and chopped nuts.

> *"This is a recipe that was brought to class during one of our student demonstrations. It's rich and luscious."*

Janet Griffith   **Norco High School, Norco, CA**

Brownie Macaroon Torte

Serves 12

Brownie:
1 (1 pound 5.5 ounce) package Pillsbury Traditional Fudge Brownie Mix
½ cup butter or margarine, softened
3 tablespoons amaretto*
2 eggs
⅓ cup miniature semi-sweet chocolate chips
Filling:
1 ½ cups coconut
½ cup almonds, toasted, finely chopped or ground**
2 tablespoons Pillsbury BEST All Purpose Flour
½ cup sweetened condensed milk
½ teaspoon almond extract
1 egg
Vanilla Glaze:
¼ cup Pillsbury Creamy Supreme Vanilla Frosting
1 tablespoon amaretto*
Chocolate Glaze:
⅓ cup semi-sweet chocolate chips
2 tablespoons whipping cream
1 ½ teaspoons butter or margarine
Garnish: 3 tablespoons sliced almonds, toasted**

Heat oven to 350 degrees. Grease bottom only of 10" springform pan. In large bowl, combine all brownie ingredients except chips; beat at low speed until moistened. Beat 1 minute at medium speed. Stir in chocolate chips. In medium bowl, combine all filling ingredients; blend well. Spoon and spread brownie batter into greased pan. With small spatula or back of spoon, make 1" wide, ½" deep circular groove in batter, about 1" from edge of pan. Make another circular groove 1" from first groove. Spoon filling into grooves; press filling in gently to same level as brownie batter. Bake 55 to 60 minutes or until center is set. Cool 15 minutes. Remove sides of pan. Refrigerate 1 ½ hours or until completely cooled. In small bowl, combine vanilla glaze ingredients; blend until smooth. Drizzle over top of torte. In small saucepan, combine all chocolate glaze ingredients. Cook over low heat 2 to 3 minutes, stirring constantly until melted and smooth. Drizzle chocolate glaze over vanilla glaze. Sprinkle top with sliced almonds.
*To substitute for 3 tablespoons amaretto, use 1 ½ teaspoons almond extract + water to equal 3 tablespoons. For 1 tablespoon amaretto, use ½ teaspoon almond extract + water to equal 1 tablespoon.
**To toast almonds, spread on cookie sheet. Bake at 350 degrees for 5 to 10 minutes or until light golden brown, stirring occasionally. Or, spread in thin layer in microwave-safe pie pan. Microwave on HIGH 5 to 7 minutes or until light golden brown, stirring frequently.

Pillsbury   **Minneapolis, MN**

Buche de Noel

Serves 12

Cake:

1 cup walnuts
¼ cup flour
¼ cup unsweetened cocoa powder
5 large eggs, separated
½ teaspoon salt
¼ teaspoon cream of tartar
⅔ cup sugar
½ teaspoon vanilla
powdered sugar

Filling:

1 cup heavy whipping cream
¼ cup powdered sugar
¼ cup candied cherries, finely chopped
½ teaspoon vanilla

Glaze:

2 teaspoons unsweetened cocoa
2 teaspoons butter, melted
1 ½ teaspoons boiling water
1 tablespoon light corn syrup
¾ cup powdered sugar, sifted

Preheat oven to 350 degrees. Grate walnuts in food processor to a fine meal. Mix with flour and cocoa; set aside. Beat egg whites to soft peak stage. Add salt and cream of tartar and continue beating to the hard peak stage; beat in ⅓ cup sugar. With same beater, beat egg yolks and remaining ⅓ cup sugar and vanilla; beat until thick. Pour egg yolks over egg white mixture and gently fold together. Gradually fold in walnut mixture. Turn into a 10" x 15" x 1" jelly roll pan lined on the bottom with greased waxed paper. Bake 20 minutes until top springs back when lightly touched. Turn out onto cloth sprinkled heavily with powdered sugar and vanilla. Roll up in cloth; allow to cool. Filling: Beat heavy cream until stiff, add powdered sugar, fold in candied cherries. Gently unroll the cooled cake and spread whipped cream mixture inside; reroll. Glaze: Mix unsweetened cocoa with butter and boiling water. Stir in light corn syrup and sifted powdered sugar. Pour over rolled cake and allow to run down sides.

NOTE: For a beautiful garnish - take 2 leaves from a rose bush or Camellia; wash, dry. Melt ¼ cup chocolate chips. Brush on top of leaf - freeze. Peel leaf off, place a cluster of sliced cherries on top of log, add chocolate leaves; gives a fancy and elegant touch!

"Great dessert for holidays."

Colleen Easton   **Brea Olinda High School, Brea, CA**

Candy Bar Bombe

Serves 8 - 9

> 6 Heath or Nestlé Crunch bars, crushed
> 1 cup whipping cream
> 2 tablespoons powdered sugar
> 1 package lady fingers
> Garnish: chocolate curls or shavings

Place candy bars in a heavy plastic bag and crush with a rolling pin; set aside. Chill whipping cream and bowl in freezer for 10 minutes. Whip the cream until it forms soft mounds. Gradually add powdered sugar and continue to whip until cream holds stiff peaks. Fold crushed candy bars into whipped cream. Place a layer of ladyfingers in an 8" x 8" dish; cover with a layer of whipped cream. Continue layering ladyfingers and whipped cream, ending with whipped cream on top. Refrigerate 6 hours before serving. Garnish with chocolate curls or shavings.

> *"I found this in a cookbook that had been printed but the title on the book was incorrectly spelled MAID, instead of MADE. Regardless, the dessert is wonderful!"*

Karen E. Jones   **Corona High School, Corona, CA**

Candy Cane Coffee Cake

Makes 2

> 2 ¼ teaspoons yeast
> ¼ cup warm water
> 1 cup sour cream
> 2 tablespoons butter
> 3 tablespoons sugar
> 1 teaspoon salt
> 1 egg
> 3 cups flour
> 1 cup canned pie filling (apple, peach, blueberry or cherry)
> 1 tablespoon butter, melted
> *Icing:*
> 2 cups powdered sugar
> 2 tablespoons water
> Candies, for decoration

Dissolve yeast in warm water for 5 minutes. Heat sour cream in microwave for 30 seconds. Stir warm sour cream into yeast. Add butter, sugar, salt, egg and 1 cup flour. Beat until smooth using mixer or wooden spoon. Mix in enough remaining flour to make dough soft and easy to handle. Turn dough onto well-floured counter and knead for about 10 minutes. Place in a greased bowl and cover. (If desired, at this point, you may place dough in greased bowl, cover with plastic wrap and place in refrigerator overnight.) Let rise in warm place 1 hour or until about doubled in size. Preheat oven to 375 degrees. Punch dough down and divide into 2 equal parts. Roll each into a rectangle 12" x 6". Place on a greased cookie sheet. With scissors, make 2" cuts every ½" on long sides of rectangles. Spread ½ cup fruit mixture down center of each rectangle. Criss cross strips over filling and pinch at ends. Stretch dough to about 16", tuck ends under. Bake 15 to 20 minutes or until golden brown. Stir together powdered sugar and 2 tablespoons water. While coffee cake is warm, brush with melted butter and drizzle with thin icing. Decorate with candies.

Charlotte Runyan   **Saddleback High School, Santa Ana, CA**

Caramel Nut Pound Cake

Serves 12 - 14
- 1 cup butter
- ½ cup shortening
- 2 cups brown sugar
- 1 cup sugar
- 5 eggs
- ½ teaspoon baking powder
- ½ teaspoon salt
- 3 cups flour, sifted
- 1 cup milk
- 1 tablespoon vanilla
- 1 cup pecans, finely chopped

Preheat oven to 325 degrees. Cream butter, shortening and brown sugar thoroughly. Gradually add sugar and continue creaming. Add eggs, one at a time, beating thoroughly after each addition. Sift baking powder and salt with flour; add alternately with milk, beginning and ending with flour. Add vanilla, then nuts and blend well. Turn batter into a well-greased and floured 10" tube or bundt pan. Bake 90 minutes. Cool in pan 15 minutes before turning out.

"Can be made ahead of time, as flavor improves with age."

Mary Lash   **Paramount High School, Paramount, CA**

Carol's Mandarin Orange Cake

Serves 8 - 12
Cake:
- 1 Duncan Hines Butter Yellow cake mix
- ½ cup oil
- 4 eggs
- juice from 1 (10 ounce) can mandarin oranges
- 2 (10 ounce) cans mandarin oranges, divided
- 1 cup nuts, chopped

Topping:
- 1 (3 ⅜ ounce) box instant vanilla pudding
- 1 medium Cool Whip
- 1 (16 ounce) can crushed pineapple, undrained

Preheat oven to 350 degrees. In a large bowl, mix cake mix with oil, eggs and mandarin orange juice. Fold in 1 ½ cans mandarin oranges and chopped nuts. Pour into 9" x 13" pan and bake 35 minutes; cool. Topping: Mix pudding with Cool Whip and crushed pineapple. Frost cooled cake and decorate top with remaining ½ can mandarin oranges.

"Everyone at RMS loves Carol's cakes! Thanks to Carol Stephenson for sharing this delicious recipe."

Rhonda Nelson   **Rancho Santa Margarita Intermediate School**
Rancho Santa Margarita, CA

Carrot Cake

Serves 12 - 15

Cake:
2 cups flour
2 cups sugar
1 teaspoon baking powder
1 teaspoon baking soda
1 teaspoon ground cinnamon
3 cups carrots, shredded
1 cup oil
4 eggs

Cream Cheese Frosting:
2 (3 ounce) packages cream cheese
½ cup margarine or butter, softened
2 teaspoons vanilla
4 ½ to 4 ¾ cups sifted powdered sugar

Preheat oven to 350 degrees. Cake: In a bowl, combine flour, sugar, baking powder, baking soda and cinnamon. Add carrot, oil and eggs. Beat with an electric mixer until combined. Pour into 2 greased and floured (9" x 1 ½") round baking pans or 1 (13" x 9") oblong pan. Bake 30 to 35 minutes, or until toothpick inserted near center comes out clean. Cool on wire racks for 10 minutes. Remove cake from pan(s). Cool thoroughly on racks. Frosting: In a bowl, beat together cream cheese, margarine or butter and vanilla until light and fluffy. Gradually beat in enough remaining powdered sugar to make frosting of spreading consistency. Frost tops and sides of cake. Cover and store in refrigerator.

> *"This is my family and friends favorite dessert recipe.*
> *I double the frosting recipe because they love it so much."*

Debi Weiss   Ayala High School, Chino Hills, CA

Carrot Cake With Pecans

Serves 8

Cake:
2 cups raisins
1 ¾ cups sugar
5 eggs
1 ½ cups corn oil
2 ½ cups flour
1 teaspoon salt
2 teaspoons baking soda
1 teaspoon cinnamon
½ cup pecans, chopped
1 ⅓ cups apples, chopped
3 cups carrots, grated

Cream Cheese Icing:
1 (8 ounce) package cream cheese
¼ cup butter, softened
2 ½ cups powdered sugar, sifted
1 teaspoon vanilla

Preheat oven to 350 degrees. Soak raisins in warm water and let stand 5 minutes; drain in a colander. (Use paper towel to blot out excess water). Beat sugar and egg together. Slowly add corn oil. Sift together flour, salt, baking soda and cinnamon; add to sugar mixture. Combine pecans, apples, carrots and raisins. Add to batter and mix well on slow speed until just combined. Pour into a greased and floured 9" x 13" pan. Bake 45 minutes or until done. Cool. Cream Cheese Frosting: Place cream cheese, butter, sugar, and vanilla in mixing bowl and beat until smooth. Spread over cooled cake.

Diana Lee   **David A. Brown Middle School, Wildomar, CA**

Carrot Pound Cake

Serves 8 - 10
Cake:
1 cup butter
1 (16 ounce) box powdered sugar
6 eggs
3 cups all-purpose flour
1 ½ teaspoons baking soda
1 teaspoon salt
2 teaspoons cinnamon
3 cups carrots, grated
¼ cup wheat germ
1 ½ cup pecans, chopped
1 tablespoon lemon juice
1 tablespoon vanilla
Lemon Glaze:
2 tablespoons butter
2 tablespoons lemon juice
½ teaspoon vanilla
1 ¼ cups powdered sugar

Preheat oven to 325 degrees. Cream butter; gradually add powdered sugar, beating well at medium speed with electric mixer. Add eggs, one at a time, beating after each addition. Combine flour, soda, salt and cinnamon and add to creamed mixture; blend well. Fold in carrots, wheat germ, pecans, lemon juice and vanilla. Spoon batter into a greased bundt pan and bake 70 minutes. Lemon Glaze: Melt butter, add lemon juice, vanilla and powdered sugar and mix until smooth. Drizzle over warm pound cake. Dust with powdered sugar, if desired.
"This is great as a dessert or breakfast snack!"
Michelle Garewal   **Los Banos High School, Los Banos, CA**

Cherimoya Passion Fruit Fluff

Serves 10 - 12
2 cups ripe cherimoya pulp
2 cups crushed pineapple, drained
2 cups passion fruit pulp
1 banana, mashed
2 cups whipping cream, whipped
10 to 12 raspberries, fresh or frozen

Scoop out pulp from cherimoyas into large bowl; remove seeds. Gently mash pulp with fork.

Add pineapple, passion fruit pulp (with or without seeds). Add mashed banana. Stir until fruits are blended. Fold in whipped cream. Divide between 10 to 12 parfait glasses. Top with raspberry. Refrigerate or serve immediately.

"Look for cherimoyas in supermarkets between November and May. Passion fruits are available year round, depending on your store. Leaving seeds in makes dessert taste more tropical."

Gloria Francuch   **Carpinteria High School, Carpinteria, CA**

Cherry Fantasy
Serves 8

- 1 can Eagle brand milk
- 1 small carton Cool Whip
- 1 can cherry pie filling
- 1 can pineapple, crushed, drained
- 1 cup pecans, chopped
- 1 cup coconut
- 1 cup miniature marshmallows

Mix Eagle brand milk and Cool Whip together. Add remaining ingredients and refrigerate for 1 hour before serving.

"Delicious! Great for the holidays. My sister, Roz, gave me this recipe and I've been making it ever since. You'll enjoy it too."

Sharron Maurice   **Blythe Middle School, Blythe, CA**

Chocolate Bottom Mini Cupcakes
Makes 3 dozen

Filling:
- 4 ounces cream cheese, softened
- 1 egg
- 3 tablespoons sugar
- ⅛ teaspoon salt
- ½ cup semi-sweet chocolate chips

Batter:
- ½ cup water
- 3 tablespoons oil
- 1 ½ teaspoons vinegar
- ½ teaspoon vanilla
- ¾ cup all-purpose flour
- ½ cup sugar
- 2 tablespoons baking cocoa
- ½ teaspoon baking soda
- ½ teaspoon salt

Preheat oven to 350 degrees. Filling: In a mixing bowl, beat cream cheese, egg, sugar and salt until smooth. Stir in chocolate chips; set aside. Batter: Combine water, oil, vinegar and vanilla in large mixing bowl. In a separate bowl, combine remaining ingredients, then add to liquid mixture; beat well (batter will be thin). Spoon about 2 teaspoons batter into well greased or paper-lined miniature muffin cups. Top with about 1 teaspoon filling. Bake 18 to 23 minutes or until a toothpick inserted in chocolate portion comes out clean. Cool 10 minutes, then remove to wire racks to cool completely.

Gale Hooper   **Casa Roble High School, Orangevale, CA**

13

Chocolate Cake Squares

Serves 12

Cake:

2 cups flour
2 cups sugar
1 cup water
4 tablespoons cocoa
½ cup margarine
½ cup vegetable shortening
2 eggs, beaten
1 teaspoon baking soda
½ cup buttermilk

Frosting:

½ cup margarine
4 tablespoons cocoa
⅓ cup milk
1 pound powdered sugar
1 teaspoon vanilla
1 cup pecans, chopped

Preheat oven to 375 degrees. Sift together flour and sugar. In a saucepan, combine and bring to a boil the water, cocoa, margarine and shortening. Add to flour mixture; stir until well blended. Add eggs, one at a time. Dissolve soda in buttermilk and add to cake mixture. Pour into a greased 9" x 13" x 2" pan. Bake 25 to 30 minutes. While cake is baking, prepare frosting. In a saucepan, combine and bring to a boil, margarine, cocoa and milk. Blend in powdered sugar. Add vanilla and chopped pecans. Spread on cake as soon as you remove from oven, while hot.

"I have used this recipe for over 40 years. It is one of the first things I learned to cook."
Dotti Jones   **Etiwanda High School, Etiwanda, CA**

Chocolate Chip Applesauce Cake

Serves 10 - 12

2 cups flour
1 ½ cups sugar
1 ½ teaspoons baking soda
1 tablespoon cocoa
1 ½ teaspoons ground allspice
1 ½ teaspoons ground nutmeg
1 ½ teaspoons ground cloves
1 teaspoon salt
½ cup shortening
2 cups applesauce
2 eggs
1 cup walnuts, chopped, divided
1 cup chocolate chips, divided
1 cup raisins
2 tablespoons brown sugar

Preheat oven to 350 degrees. In a large mixing bowl, combine the first 8 ingredients; mix well. Add shortening, applesauce, eggs, ½ cup chopped nuts, ½ cup chocolate chips and raisins; beat until well blended. Pour batter into a greased 13" x 9" x 2" pan. Sprinkle top of batter with brown sugar, remaining walnuts and chocolate chips. Bake 45 to 50 minutes or until cake tests done. Cut into squares to serve.

Astrid Curfman   **Newcomb Academy, Long Beach, CA**

Chocolate Chipper Cake
Serves 8 - 12

- 1 large package chocolate pudding mix (not instant)
- 3 cups nonfat milk
- 1 box chocolate cake mix
- 1 package semi-sweet chocolate chips

Preheat oven to 350 degrees. Cook chocolate pudding with nonfat milk according to package directions. As soon as it boils, remove from heat and add cake mix. Mix until cake mix is blended. Pour mixture in 9" x 13" pan, greased and floured; then sprinkle chocolate chips over top. Bake 30 minutes.

"This is the easiest and best chocolate fix for all! It doesn't require much preparation time and therefore makes it easy to make for a lab or for any last minute functions."

Jeanette Moule   **Central Valley High School, Shasta Lake City, CA**

Chocolate Coffee Cake
Serves 10-12

- ½ pound margarine
- 1 cup sugar
- 2 eggs
- 2 cups flour
- 1 teaspoon baking soda
- 1 teaspoon baking powder
- 1 teaspoon vanilla
- 1 cup sour cream
- ½ package chocolate chips
- 2 tablespoons cocoa
- 5 tablespoons milk
- 1 teaspoon cinnamon
- ¼ cup walnuts, chopped
- ½ cup brown sugar

Preheat oven to 350 degrees. Cream butter and sugar; add eggs and beat well. Add dry ingredients and sour cream and vanilla. In a small saucepan, melt chocolate chips with cocoa and milk. In another bowl, stir together cinnamon, walnuts and brown sugar. Pour half of the brown sugar mixture into cake batter and pour batter into greased pan. Put half the melted chocolate mixture on top of batter and marbleize batter. Sprinkle with remaining brown sugar mixture and drizzle remaining chocolate mixture on top. Bake 1 hour.

"Delicious cake - a long time family favorite."

Marlene Meola   **Norte Vista High School, Riverside, CA**

Chocolate Eclair Cake

Serves 12

1 (6 ounce) box instant French vanilla pudding
3 cups milk
1 (8 ounce) carton Cool Whip
1 (16 ounce) box graham crackers
Icing:
3 tablespoons + 1 ½ teaspoons margarine, melted
5 tablespoons cocoa
3 tablespoons milk
1 tablespoon vanilla
2 tablespoons light corn syrup
1 ½ cups powdered sugar, sifted

Mix pudding, milk and Cool Whip until well blended. In a buttered 9" x 13" pan, place 1 layer of graham crackers, ½ of the pudding mixture, a second layer of graham crackers, the rest of the pudding mixture, then top with a 3rd layer of graham crackers. Icing: Mix melted margarine and cocoa to form a paste. Add milk and vanilla slowly while stirring to keep mixture smooth. Add corn syrup and sifted powdered sugar and stir until smooth and creamy. Spread icing on top layer of graham crackers. Refrigerate several hours or overnight. Cut with a knife dipped in warm water.

"This recipe was very popular when used for the "Honors Dessert" at Brea Olinda High School."

Paula Skrifvars   **Brea Junior High School, Brea, CA**

Chocolate Raspberry Pound Cake

Serves 12

1 cup seedless black raspberry preserves, divided
2 cups flour
1 ½ cups sugar
¾ cup cocoa
1 ½ teaspoons baking soda
1 teaspoon salt
⅔ cup butter or margarine, softened
1 (16 ounce) carton sour cream
2 eggs
1 teaspoon vanilla extract
powdered sugar
Raspberry Cream:
1 (10 ounce) package frozen red raspberries in light syrup
8 ounces whipped topping, thawed

Preheat oven to 350 degrees. Grease and flour a 12 cup bundt pan. In microwave safe bowl, place ¾ cup preserves. Microwave on HIGH 30 to 45 seconds, or until melted; cool. In large bowl, stir together flour, sugar, cocoa, baking soda and salt. Add butter, sour cream, eggs, vanilla and melted preserves. Beat on medium speed of electric mixer 3 to 4 minutes until well blended. Pour batter into prepared pan and bake 50 to 60 minutes, until toothpick inserted in center comes out clean. Cool 10 minutes; remove from pan to wire rack. Place remaining ¼ cup preserves in small microwave safe bowl. Microwave on HIGH 30 seconds, or until melted; brush over warm cake; cool completely. Raspberry Cream: Place thawed raspberries with syrup in food processor or blender. Strain into medium bowl, discarding seeds. Blend whipped topping with raspberry purée. At serving time, sprinkle cake with powdered sugar over top. Fill center with Raspberry Cream.

Joy Sweeney-Aiello　　　　　　　　　　　　　**Liberty High School, Brentwood, CA**

Chocolate Zucchini Sheet Cake

Serves 20

Cake:
2 cups sugar
1 cup vegetable oil
3 eggs
2 ½ cups all-purpose flour
¼ cup baking cocoa
1 teaspoon baking soda
¼ teaspoon baking powder
¼ teaspoon salt
½ cup milk
2 cups fresh zucchini, shredded
1 tablespoon vanilla extract

Frosting:
¼ cup butter
¼ cup cocoa
6 tablespoons evaporated milk
1 pound powdered sugar
1 tablespoon vanilla

Preheat oven to 375 degrees. In large mixing bowl, combine sugar and oil. Add eggs, one at a time, beating well after each addition. Combine flour, cocoa, baking soda, baking powder and salt. Gradually add to egg mixture alternately, with milk. Stir in zucchini and vanilla. Pour into a greased 15" x 10" pan and bake 25 minutes. Frosting: Beat together frosting ingredients until smooth. When cake is done, remove from oven and frost while cake is hot.

"This is a good way to use all that zucchini! This cake is very moist and delicious. I got it from Country magazine several years ago. Guests love it!"

Marty Parker　　　　　　　　　　　　　**Poway High School, Poway, CA**

Chocolate-Caramel-Pecan Squares

Serves 15

1 package Betty Crocker Super Moist chocolate fudge cake mix
¾ cup water
¼ cup vegetable oil
3 eggs
1 (12 ounce) jar caramel ice cream topping
½ cup pecans, toasted, chopped
Ice cream

Heat oven to 350 degrees. Toast pecans in an ungreased baking sheet for about 10 minutes, stirring occasionally, until golden brown. Grease a 15 ½" x 10 ½" x 1" jelly roll pan, with shortening; lightly flour. Beat cake mix together with water, oil and eggs in large bowl on low speed 30 seconds. Beat on medium speed 2 minutes. Pour batter into pan. Drizzle half of the caramel topping (about ½ cup) evenly over batter. Sprinkle with pecans. Bake 25 to 30 minutes or until cake springs back when touched lightly in center; cool slightly. Heat remaining caramel topping over low heat, stirring constantly, until heated through. Cut warm cake into 3" squares. Serve with ice cream and warm caramel topping.

General Mills   **Minneapolis, MN**

Chocolate-Kahlua Bundt Cake

Serves 6-8

1 package chocolate cake mix
1 (8 ounce) carton sour cream
1 package chocolate chips
2 eggs
¼ cup vegetable oil
½ cup Kahlua

Preheat oven to 375 degrees. Mix all ingredients together in a bowl. Grease and flour a bundt pan, pour in batter and bake 50 minutes. (NOTE: Toothpick test does not work on this cake.) Invert onto serving platter. If desired, sift a fine layer of powdered sugar over top for garnish.

"Mix in one bowl, bake in bundt pan - easy, easy, easy and SO rich."

Amy Bean   **Cabrillo High School, Lompoc, CA**

Cinnamon Chocolate Cake

Serves 24

Cake:
2 cups flour
2 cups sugar
1 teaspoon cinnamon
1 stick margarine or butter
4 teaspoons cocoa
1 cup water
½ cup shortening
½ cup buttermilk
1 teaspoon baking soda
2 eggs
2 teaspoons vanilla
Icing:
1 stick margarine
2 tablespoons cocoa
6 tablespoons milk
1 pound powdered sugar
1 teaspoon vanilla
1 teaspoon cinnamon
1 cup walnuts, chopped
1 cup coconut

Preheat oven to 400 degrees. In mixing bowl, combine flour, sugar and cinnamon; set aside. In saucepan, heat margarine, cocoa, water and shortening to boiling; pour over dry ingredients. Add buttermilk, baking soda, eggs and vanilla; mix well. Pour into a 11" x 15" x 3" jelly-roll pan and bake 20 minutes. Icing: In a saucepan, combine margarine, cocoa and milk; heat to boiling. Remove from heat; add powdered sugar a little at a time, stirring thoroughly. Add vanilla, cinnamon, walnuts and coconut. Spread over cake while still warm.

"Tastes wonderful!"

Olga Sarouhan   **Edison High School, Huntington Beach, CA**

Cocoa Apple Cake

Serves 8 - 10

      3 eggs
      2 cups sugar
      1 cup shortening
      ½ cup water
      2 ¼ cups flour, unsifted
      2 tablespoons cocoa
      1 teaspoon baking soda
      1 teaspoon cinnamon
      1 teaspoon allspice
      1 cup nuts, chopped
      ½ cup chocolate chips
      2 apples, cored and grated (2 cups)
      1 tablespoon vanilla
      1 cup raisins (optional)

Preheat oven to 325 degrees. Beat together eggs, sugar, shortening and water until fluffy. Stir together dry ingredients and spices. Add to creamed mixture and mix well. Fold in nuts, chocolate chips, apples, vanilla and raisins until evenly distributed. Spoon into greased and floured tube or bundt cake pan. Bake 60 to 70 minutes, or until cake tests done. Cool in pan 15 minutes before turning onto a wire rack to complete cooling.

"I plump the raisins by pouring boiling water over them and then draining them just before adding into the cake batter."

Katherine Iverson   **Vandenberg Middle School, Lompoc, CA**

Colonial Poppy Seed Cake

Serves 6 - 8

      ½ cup poppy seeds
      ¾ cup milk
      ¾ cup (1 ½ sticks) butter, softened
      3 eggs
      1 cup sugar
      1 teaspoon vanilla
      2 teaspoons baking powder
      2 cups sifted all-purpose flour
      Powdered sugar

Preheat oven to 350 degrees. Combine poppy seeds and milk in large bowl. Let stand at room temperature 3 to 4 hours. Let butter and eggs warm to room temperature for easy mixing. Grease and flour a loaf pan. Add butter, eggs, sugar, vanilla, baking powder and flour to poppy seeds and milk. Beat at medium speed with mixer for 1 minute. Pour into prepared pan. Bake for 1 hour and 15 minutes, or until center springs back. Cool in pan on rack 5 minutes; loosen, then turn out to cool. Sprinkle with powdered sugar.

"This is one of my favorite recipes. It's like a pound cake which is a cross between a cake and a bread. Try it toasted with butter along with a cup of coffee or tea."

Sheryl Malone   **Mt. Carmel High School, San Diego, CA**

Cranberry Cake
Serves 10 - 12

3 eggs
2 cups sugar
¾ cup butter or margarine, softened
1 teaspoon almond extract
2 cups all purpose flour
2 ½ cups fresh or frozen cranberries, thawed
⅔ cup pecans, chopped
Whipped cream (optional)

Preheat oven to 350 degrees. In a mixing bowl, beat eggs with sugar until slightly thickened and light in color, about 5 minutes. Add butter and almond extract; beat 2 minutes. Stir in flour just until combined. Stir in cranberries and pecans. Spread in greased 13" x 9" x 2" pan and bake 45 to 50 minutes or until wooden pick inserted near center comes out clean. Serve with whipped cream.

"We like this recipe so much that I buy extra bags of cranberries and freeze them so that I can make the recipe throughout the year."

Ramona Erickson   **Highland High School, Palmdale, CA**

Cranberry Delight
Serves 4 - 6

½ cup sugar
1 cup flour
1 ½ teaspoons baking powder
½ cup milk
1 ½ tablespoons butter, melted
1 cup raw cranberries
Sauce:
1 cup sugar
1 tablespoon flour
½ cup evaporated milk
1 ½ sticks butter
1 teaspoon vanilla
pinch salt

Preheat oven to 375 degrees. Sift together first 3 ingredients. Add milk, melted butter and cranberries. Pour into an 8" x 8" pan and bake 30 minutes. Sauce: Mix sugar and flour together; add evaporated milk, butter, vanilla and salt; bring to a boil and cook 15 minutes. Cut cake into serving sizes and spoon warm sauce over.

"This is a family favorite. We serve it every year at Christmas!"

Judy Hammann   **Mesa Junior High School, Mesa, CA**

Crazy Cake

Serves 8 - 12

  3 cups flour
  2 cups sugar
  ⅓ cup cocoa
  2 teaspoons baking soda
  1 teaspoon salt
  2 tablespoons vinegar
  1 teaspoon vanilla
  ¾ cup oil
  2 cups cold water

Preheat oven to 350 degrees. Mix first 5 ingredients together in a 9" x 13" cake pan. Make 3 wells in dry ingredients. Place vinegar in first hole, vanilla and oil in second hole and water in third hole. Mix until well blended. Bake 30 to 35 minutes.

  "Great when you want to bake a cake and find you have no eggs. Low in saturated fat!"
Linda Mastri   **Durango High School, Las Vegas, NV**

Cream Filled Cupcakes

Makes 16 - 20

  1 package chocolate cake mix, prepared
  1 (8 ounce) package cream cheese
  ⅓ cup sugar
  1 egg
  1 cup chocolate chips

Prepare cake mix batter according to directions. Fill cupcake papers ⅔ full. In separate bowl, mix cream cheese, sugar and egg together and blend until smooth. Stir in chocolate chips. Place 1 rounded teaspoon of cream cheese mixture on top of each cupcake and bake as directed on cake mix package.

  "The cream cheese will sink when baked which makes a frosting-like filling
  when you bite into the cupcake. So moist, there is no need for frosting."
Trena Becker   **Ball Junior High School, Anaheim, CA**

Cream Puff Cake

Serves 8 - 10

½ cup margarine
1 cup water
1 cup flour
4 eggs
2 (3 ounce) packages instant vanilla pudding
1 (8 ounce) package cream cheese, softened
3 cups milk
1 large Cool Whip
chocolate syrup

Preheat oven to 400 degrees. Bring margarine and water to a boil in saucepan. Stir in flour and beat until mixture forms a ball. Add eggs, one at a time, beating until smooth. Spread batter in a 13" x 9" pan and bake 30 minutes until puffed and golden; cool. Beat together pudding mix, cream cheese and milk. Spread over crust, then spread Cool Whip over pudding. Drizzle chocolate syrup on top. Refrigerate until serving.

"Tastes just like a cream puff, but easier to make! Yum!"

Penny Niadna   **Golden West High School, Visalia, CA**

Crunchy Brunch Cake

Serves 12

¾ cup Wheaties cereal, coarsely crushed (about 1 ½ cups uncrushed)
½ teaspoon ground cinnamon
1 package Betty Crocker One-Step White Angel Food Cake Mix
Serving Ideas (below)

Move oven rack to lowest position. Heat to 350 degrees. Mix cereal and cinnamon. Prepare cake mix as directed on package, except fold cereal mixture into batter. Pour into ungreased 12 cup bundt cake pan. Bake as directed. Immediately turn pan upside down onto heatproof funnel. Let stand 2 hours or until completely cool. Remove from pan. Serve with one or more serving ideas.

Serving Ideas: Lowfat yogurt (strawberry, peach, banana); fresh or frozen (thawed) fruit (strawberries, peaches, bananas); Wheaties cereal; raisins; nuts.

General Mills   **Minneapolis, MN**

Deanna's Delight

Serves 10 - 12

Crust:
1 cup flour
½ cup butter
1 cup nuts, chopped
Cream cheese layer:
1 cup powdered sugar
8 ounces cream cheese
1 cup Cool Whip
Pudding layer:
2 cups milk
1 small box instant vanilla pudding mix, prepared with milk
1 small box instant chocolate pudding mix, prepared with milk
Topping:
8 ounces Cool Whip
2 tablespoons nuts, chopped

Preheat oven to 350 degrees. Mix flour, butter and chopped nuts and spread in 9" x 13" pan. Bake 20 minutes; cool. Combine powdered sugar, cream cheese and Cool Whip with electric mixer. Spread carefully onto crust. Prepare vanilla pudding as directed on package and spread over cream cheese layer. Prepare chocolate pudding as directed on package and spread over vanilla pudding layer. Spread Cool whip over all and sprinkle with nuts.

"This can be low fat, low sugar, by using light cream cheese,
light Cool Whip and light pudding mixes."

Elizabeth Thornburg   **Selma High School, Selma, CA**

Devil's Food Cake

Serves 12

¾ cup cocoa
1 cup boiling water
2 cups sugar
¾ cup butter
2 eggs
1 teaspoon vanilla
1 teaspoon baking soda
2 ½ cups flour
1 cup buttermilk

Preheat oven to 350 degrees. Grease 2 (8") cake pans. Dissolve cocoa in boiling water; cool. Cream sugar and butter with electric mixer on medium speed until light and fluffy, about 1 minute. Add eggs and vanilla, blending well, about 2 minutes. Stir in cocoa mixture. Add baking soda and flour alternately with buttermilk, mixing well after each addition, 2 to 3 minutes. Pour into pans and bake 30 to 35 minutes. Frost with desired frosting.

"This recipe was given to me by a very good friend of my husband's,
and I bake it for him every year for his birthday!"

Carol O'Keefe   **Canyon High School, Anaheim, CA**

Double Cherry Dessert

Serves 12

1 package Cherry Chip Cake mix
2 eggs
½ cup margarine, softened
1 can cherry pie filling
½ cup pecans, chopped
Vanilla Glaze:
1 cup powdered sugar
1 tablespoon water

Preheat oven to 350 degrees. Mix dry cake mix with eggs and margarine until smooth. Spread in an ungreased 13" x 9" x 2" pan. Spread pie filling over and sprinkle with pecans. Bake until browned, 55 to 60 minutes. Cool 15 minutes. Glaze: Mix powdered sugar with water, adding additional water if necessary, to make a thin glaze. Drizzle cake with glaze.

"This is a quick and delicious dessert that's similar to a coffeecake."

Linda Stroup   **Virgin Valley High School, Mesquite, NV**

Dump Cake

Serves 6 - 8

1 can Comstock apple pie filling
1 (16 ounce) can crushed pineapple, with juice
1 box cake mix, white or yellow
¼ cup butter or margarine, melted
½ cup nuts, chopped
Garnish: whipped cream

Preheat oven to 350 degrees. Using a 9" x 13" pan, spread pie filling in bottom, top with pineapple and juice, sprinkle dry cake mix on top, spreading over evenly. Pour melted butter evenly over dry cake mix and top with nuts. Bake 30 minutes.

"Serve topped with whipped cream."

Carolyn Helmle   **Thomas Downey High School, Modesto, CA**

Earthquake Cake

Serves 10 - 12

1 cup pecans or walnuts, chopped
1 cup shredded coconut
1 German chocolate cake mix; prepared according to package directions
1 (8 ounce) package cream cheese, softened
½ cup margarine
1 pound powdered sugar
1 teaspoon vanilla

Preheat oven to 350 degrees. Place pecans and coconut in bottom of greased 9" x 13" baking dish. Prepare German chocolate cake according to package directions. Pour prepared batter over nuts and coconut. In a large bowl, mix cream cheese, margarine, powdered sugar and vanilla until smooth. Carefully spoon over unbaked batter. Bake 45 to 50 minutes.

Bonnie Landin   **Garden Grove High School, Garden Grove, CA**

Easy Black Forest Cake

Serves 12

Cake:
1 package Devil's Food cake mix
1 (21 ounce) can cherry pie filling
1 teaspoon almond extract
2 eggs, beaten
Frosting:
1 cup sugar
5 teaspoons butter
⅓ cup milk
1 (6 ounce) package semi-sweet chocolate chips

Preheat oven to 350 degrees. Mix together cake ingredients and put in greased and floured 9" x 13" pan. Bake 25 to 30 minutes. Frosting. Combine sugar, butter and milk in saucepan. Boil one minute, stirring constantly. Remove from heat and stir in chocolate chips. Blend until smooth and pour over cake.

Gayle Grigg   **Hendrix Junior High School, Chandler, AZ**

Erna's Best Chocolate Cake & Frosting

Serves 12

3 squares unsweetened chocolate
½ cup butter
2 ¼ cups brown sugar
3 eggs
1 ¼ teaspoons vanilla
2 ¼ cups flour
2 teaspoons baking soda
½ teaspoon salt
1 cup sour cream
1 cup boiling water
Frosting:
4 squares unsweetened chocolate
½ cup butter
1 pound powdered sugar
½ cup milk
2 teaspoons vanilla

Preheat oven to 350 degrees. Melt chocolate slowly in small bowl in microwave at 50% power, checking often to make sure chocolate doesn't burn; let cool. Grease and flour cake pans. In a mixer, beat butter. Add brown sugar and eggs and beat until light and fluffy. Add melted chocolate and vanilla. Stir in dry ingredients alternately with the sour cream. Add boiling water. Batter will be thin. Pour into pans or cupcake liners and bake 30 to 35 minutes. Frosting: Melt chocolate and butter in the microwave. In a medium bowl, combine sugar, milk and vanilla and stir until smooth. Add the chocolate mixture. Put this bowl in a larger bowl of ice and stir until frosting is firm enough to spread.

"My mom has made this cake for many of my children's birthday parties. It's a great cake loved by children and adults. It has won several blue ribbons at the Santa Barbara fair."

Debra Teton   **Goleta Valley Junior High School, Goleta, CA**

Farm Cakes

Serves 18
Cake:
3 cups flour
2 cups sugar
½ cup unsweetened cocoa powder
2 teaspoons baking soda
2 cups water
⅔ cup vegetable oil
2 tablespoons cider vinegar
2 teaspoons vanilla
Filling:
8 ounces cream cheese, softened
1 egg
⅓ cup sugar
pinch salt
6 ounces semi-sweet chocolate chips

Preheat oven to 350 degrees. Cake: Lightly grease 2 muffin tins. Sift together flour, sugar, cocoa and baking soda into large mixing bowl. Add water, oil, vinegar and vanilla and beat at medium speed for about 3 minutes, until well combined. Filling: In large bowl, using a wooden spoon, cream the cream cheese. Add egg, sugar and salt and beat until smooth and thoroughly combined; fold in chocolate chips. Pour cake batter into prepared muffin cups, filling each about ⅔ full. Spoon 2 tablespoons filling into center of each cake. Bake 20 to 25 minutes, until cakes spring back.

Liz Coleman   **Oroville High School, Oroville, CA**

Fresh Apple Cake

Serves 10 - 12
2 cups sugar
1 ½ cups oil
2 eggs, beaten
3 cups flour
1 teaspoon salt
1 teaspoon baking soda
1 teaspoon cinnamon
1 teaspoon vanilla
3 cups apples, chopped
1 cup nuts, chopped

Preheat oven to 350 degrees. Mix sugar and oil; beat in eggs. Mix in flour, salt, baking soda, cinnamon and vanilla. Fold in chopped apples and nuts. Pour into a greased 9" x 13" pan. Bake 1 hour, or until a toothpick inserted in center comes out clean.
"This is my father's favorite cake. My kids love it too!"

Cari Sheridan   **Grace Yokley School, Ontario, CA**

Gooey Butter Cake

Serves 12

- 1 yellow cake mix
- 1 egg
- 1 cube margarine, melted
- 1 pound powdered sugar
- 2 eggs
- 1 (8 ounce) package cream cheese, softened

Preheat oven 350 degrees. Mix first 3 ingredients together and spread in a 9" x 13" pan. Blend the next 3 ingredients in another bowl and beat 3 minutes. Pour over batter in pan; bake 35 to 40 minutes.

"This is a quick, easy recipe we serve around the campfire, and everyone seems to enjoy."
Joanne Montoy   **Esperanza High School, Anaheim, CA**

Heath Bar Kahlua Cake

Serves 20

- 1 chocolate cake mix, prepared according to package directions
- ½ cup Kahlua
- 2 (3.4 ounce) packages chocolate pudding
- 2 ¼ cups milk
- 1 (12 ounce) carton Cool Whip
- 2 Heath or Skor Bars, broken into small pieces

Mix and bake chocolate cake according to package directions; cool. With a toothpick, poke holes in the cake. Pour Kahlua over cake. Prepare pudding using milk. Using a large glass trifle or salad bowl, layer one half of the cake, broken into small pieces with pudding, Cool Whip and candy. Make two layers, ending with Cool Whip and candy. Refrigerate four hours.

Maggie Busch   **Eisenhower High School, Rialto, CA**

Hershey's Pick-Your-Favorite Chocolate Frosting
Makes 2 cups

6 tablespoons (¾ stick) butter or margarine, softened
2 ⅔ cups powdered sugar
½ cup Hershey's Cocoa or Hershey's European Style Cocoa
¼ cup + 1 to 2 tablespoons milk, divided
1 teaspoon vanilla

In medium bowl, beat butter. Stir together powdered sugar and cocoa; add alternately with ¼ cup milk and vanilla. Beat to spreading consistency; beat in remaining 1 to 2 tablespoons milk, if needed.

Variations: Add one of the following in addition to the vanilla extract.
Citrus Chocolate Frosting: ½ teaspoon orange extract
Maple Chocolate Frosting: ½ teaspoon maple extract
Mint Chocolate Frosting: ½ teaspoon mint or peppermint extract
Mocha Chocolate Frosting: 2 teaspoons powdered instant coffee dissolved in the milk
Peanut Butter Chocolate Frosting: 2 tablespoons Reese's Creamy Peanut Butter

Hershey Foods Corp.   **Hershey, PA**

Kahlua Chocolate Chip Cake
Serves 10 - 12

1 package chocolate cake mix
1 (3.5 ounce) package instant chocolate pudding
1 pint sour cream
½ cup Kahlua
¼ cup oil
2 eggs
1 (12 ounce) package chocolate chips

Preheat oven to 350 degrees. Mix ingredients together and pour into greased and floured bundt pan. Bake 45 to 55 minutes.

Peggy Herndon   **Central Valley High School, Shasta Lake City, CA**

Lemon Refrigerator Cake
Serves 12 - 15

1 (18 ¼ ounce) package white cake mix, prepared
1 (3 ounce) package lemon pudding mix, prepared
Grated peel and juice of 1 lemon
1 cup evaporated milk, chilled
¼ cup sugar
1 cup shredded coconut, divided

Prepare and bake cake according to package directions, using a greased and flour 13" x 9" baking pan. Cool in pan ten minutes before removing to a wire rack. Prepare pudding according to package directions. Add lemon peel; cool. In a small bowl, whip milk. Add lemon juice and sugar; blend for 30 seconds. Fold into pudding. Carefully fold in ¾ cup coconut. Split cooled cake into 2 layers. Spread pudding mixture between layers and on top. Sprinkle with remaining coconut. Store in refrigerator.

"This is a very light cake and the students love it!"

Edith B. Novascone   **Burroughs High School, Ridgecrest, CA**

Mandarin Magic Cake
Serves 12

Cake:
1 box yellow cake mix
4 eggs
½ cup oil
1 can Mandarin oranges, with juice

Frosting:
1 (9 ounce) carton whipped topping
1 (medium) can pineapple, crushed, with juice
1 box vanilla instant pudding
½ teaspoon vanilla

Preheat oven to 350 degrees. Beat cake ingredients together, about 3 minutes. Pour batter into 3 (9") cake pans which have been greased and floured. Bake until lightly browned, about 20 minutes. Cool cake. Combine frosting ingredients and spread on cooled cake. Cake should be refrigerated if not eaten the same day.

"Freezes well...very moist!"

Sybil Schweighauser   **North High School, Bakersfield, CA**

Mandarin Orange Cake
Serves 15

Cake:
2 cups flour
2 cups sugar
2 eggs
2 teaspoons baking soda
1 teaspoon salt
2 cans Mandarin oranges, well drained

Topping:
1 ½ cups brown sugar
6 tablespoons margarine
6 tablespoons milk

Preheat oven to 350 degrees. Cake: In large mixing bowl, combine all ingredients and mix well with electric mixer. Pour into ungreased 9" x 13" pan and bake 30 to 35 minutes. Topping: Mix brown sugar, margarine and milk in saucepan; bring to boil. While cake is hot, poke holes in top with a fork. Pour topping over cake. Serve warm or cool with Cool Whip or ice cream.

"Mixes up quickly for unexpected company."

Paula Schaefer   **Garside Middle School, Las Vegas, NV**

Mississippi Mud Cake

Serves 12 - 18

Cake:
2 cubes butter, melted
3 ½ tablespoonS cocoa
4 eggs
2 cups sugar
1 ½ cups flour
1 teaspoon vanilla
1 ½ cups coconut
1 jar marshmallow creme
Frosting:
1 cup butter
⅓ cup milk or evaporated milk
3 ½ tablespoons cocoa
1 box powdered sugar, sifted
Garnish: chopped walnuts

Preheat oven to 350 degrees. Mix together butter, cocoa, eggs, sugar, flour, vanilla and coconut. Spread into a greased 9" x 13" pan and bake 30 minutes. While still hot, spread 1 jar marshmallow creme over top and return to oven until melted. Remove from oven and cool. Frosting: Melt butter in small saucepan; add milk and cocoa and bring to a boil, stirring constantly, about 1 minute. Add sifted powdered sugar and blend well. Frost cake and garnish with chopped walnuts.

"Very rich but very yummy!"

Laurie Bleecker   **Centennial High School, Corona, CA**

Oatmeal Cake with Cream Cheese Frosting

Serves 12

Cake:
1 ½ cups boiling water
1 cup quick cooking oats
½ cup margarine (1 stick)
1 cup sugar
1 cup brown sugar, firmly packed
2 eggs
1 teaspoon vanilla
1 ½ cups flour
1 teaspoon baking soda
1 teaspoon cinnamon
½ teaspoon salt
Cream Cheese Frosting:
3 ounces cream cheese
1 teaspoon vanilla
1 box powdered sugar
¼ cup milk (or more)

Stir oats into boiling water; add margarine, cover pan and let set 30 minutes. Preheat oven to 350 degrees. Cream sugars, vanilla and eggs together. In another bowl, sift together flour, baking soda, cinnamon and salt; blend into creamed mixture. Stir in oatmeal mixture and mix well. Pour into a greased and floured 9" x 13" pan and bake 30 to 35 minutes. While cake cools, prepare frosting. Cream together cream cheese and vanilla. Add powdered sugar gradually. Beat all ingredients well. Add milk, 1 tablespoon at a time, until desired consistency is achieved. Frost cooled cake.

"The cooked oats adds a moist texture and flavor to make this cake delicious and healthy too! No one ever believes it has cooked oats in it."

Betty Bundy   **Hidden Valley Middle School, Escondido, CA**

Old Fashioned Banana Streusel Cake
Serves 8

½ cup unsalted butter, softened
1 ¼ cups + 2 tablespoons sugar
2 large eggs
2 teaspoons vanilla
⅓ cup buttermilk
1 ½ cups ripe bananas, puréed
1 ¾ cups cake flour
1 teaspoon baking soda
1 teaspoon baking powder
½ teaspoon salt

Preheat oven to 350 degrees. Cream butter and sugar in mixer until light and fluffy. Add eggs and beat until batter flows easily, about 3 minutes. Add vanilla, buttermilk and banana purée; mix well to combine. Sift flour, baking soda, baking powder and salt. Add gradually to batter, mixing until very smooth. Grease a 9" square pan, then coat lightly with flour. Transfer batter to pan, smooth surface with spatula and sprinkle with streusel topping evenly over surface. Bake in center of oven at 350 degrees, until medium brown and wood pick inserted in center comes out clean.

Leiann Riggins   **Villa Park High School, Villa Park, CA**

Papa Pucci's Tiramisu
Serves 8

4 (extra large) eggs, separated
1 pint whipping cream
½ cup sugar, divided
1 (16 ounce) container mascarpone cheese
1 cup espresso coffee, brewed
½ cup rum
¼ cup triple sec
Lady finger cookies
Shaved chocolate

Separate egg yolks and whites. In a large bowl, beat egg yolks, whipping cream and ¼ cup sugar until creamy. In separate bowl, beat egg whites and remaining ¼ cup sugar until soft peaks form. Fold egg white mixture into egg yolk mixture. Add mascarpone cheese and mix until well blended. In a large liquid measuring cup or bowl, mix espresso coffee, rum and triple sec. In a deep 9" x 13" pan, layer the ingredients in the following order: light layer of cream mixture; lady fingers; ⅓ espresso mixture; ⅓ cream mixture; lady fingers; repeat twice. Shave chocolate on top of last cream layer. Cover and chill overnight to set.

"This is one of my Dad's, chef Enrico Pucci's, most famous recipes.
It is authentically Italian, like my Dad!"

Alicia Pucci   **Kenilworth Junior High School, Petaluma, CA**

31

Pineapple Kiwi Cake

Serves 12

- 1 box yellow cake mix, with pudding
- 1 (20 ounce) can crushed pineapple
- 2 to 3 kiwi fruit
- 1 small box instant vanilla pudding mix
- 1 cup milk
- 1 (8 ounce) carton Cool Whip
- ¼ cup walnuts, finely chopped (optional)

Preheat oven to 350 degrees. Prepare cake mix as directed on package, using a 9" x 13" pan; cool slightly. Prick cake thoroughly. Pour crushed pineapple with juice over top of cake. Peel kiwi and slice. Place slices over pineapple. Prepare pudding as directed on package but use only 1 cup milk. Fold into Cool Whip until blended. Ice cake with pudding mixture. Sprinkle with chopped nuts. Refrigerate.

Variation: Substitute chocolate cake mix, top with cherry pie filling and chocolate chips; ice with chocolate pudding instead of vanilla.

"An absolutely delicious moist, light cake guaranteed to get rave reviews! Thanks Milo and Alice!"
Millie Deeton   **Ayala High School, Chino Hills, CA**

Pistachio Nut Cake

Serves 10 - 12

Cake:
- 1 package white cake mix
- 1 small box pistachio instant pudding mix
- 3 eggs
- 1 cup oil
- 1 cup club soda
- ½ cup pecans, chopped

Frosting:
- 1 envelope Dream Whip
- 1 small package pistachio instant pudding mix
- 1 ½ cups milk

Preheat oven to 350 degrees. Mix all cake ingredients together and beat 2 minutes on medium speed. Pour batter into a greased and floured 13" x 9" pan. Bake 50 minutes. Frosting: Beat frosting ingredients together and frost cooled cake.

Pam Fecchino   **Cimarron-Memorial High School, Las Vegas, NV**

Pumpkin Cake Roll

Serves 8

Cake:
- 3 eggs
- 1 cup sugar
- ⅔ cup pumpkin
- 1 teaspoon lemon juice
- ¾ cup flour
- 1 teaspoon baking powder

Giant Birthday Cookie

Page 77

Chocolate Chip, Oats 'n
Caramel Cookie Squares

page 68

2 teaspoons cinnamon
1 teaspoon ginger
½ teaspoon nutmeg
½ teaspoon salt
1 cup walnuts, finely chopped
½ cup powdered sugar
Filling:
1 cup powdered sugar
8 ounces lowfat cream cheese, softened
½ teaspoon vanilla

Preheat oven to 375 degrees. Beat eggs on high speed for 5 minutes. Stir in sugar, pumpkin and lemon juice. In separate bowl, mix dry ingredients and add to pumpkin mixture. Spread onto a greased and floured jelly roll pan. Top with walnuts. Bake 12 to 15 minutes. Turn out on a towel that has been sprinkled with powdered sugar. Starting at narrow end, roll towel and cake together. Cool; unroll. Filling: Combine filling ingredients and beat until smooth. Spread over unrolled cake; roll again and chill until serving. (May also be frozen)

"Tastes like cake and cheesecake rolled together."

Jill Burnham   **Bloomington High School, Bloomington, CA**

Pumpkin Cranberry Bundt Cake
Serves 12 - 16

2 ¼ cups flour
1 ½ teaspoons cinnamon
¾ teaspoon nutmeg
¼ teaspoon ginger
¼ teaspoon ground cloves
1 teaspoon baking soda
½ teaspoon salt
2 eggs
2 cups sugar
½ cup oil
1 cup puréed pumpkin
1 cup dried cranberries
Powdered sugar

Preheat oven to 350 degrees. Grease and flour bundt pan. In large bowl, combine flower, spices, baking soda and salt. Mix well and set aside. In small mixing bowl, beat eggs until foamy. Beat in sugar, oil and pumpkin purée. Add to dry ingredients. Stir until just moistened. Fold in cranberries. Pour into bundt pan. Bake 50 minutes, until toothpick inserted in center comes out clean. Cool 10 minutes; remove from pan. Cool completely. Dust with powdered sugar.

"Moist and delicious. It gets eaten so fast that I always make two!"

Cathy Miller   **Montclair High School, Montclair, CA**

Pumpkin Crunch Cake

Serves 10 - 12

    1 can Libby's pumpkin pie mix
    2 eggs
    1 (5 ounce) can evaporated milk
    1 Duncan Hines spice cake mix
    1 ⅓ sticks butter, very firm
    1 cup nuts, chopped
    Garnish: whipped cream

Preheat oven to 350 degrees. Mix together pumpkin pie mix, eggs and evaporated milk. Pour into a 9" x 13" baking pan. Sprinkle spice cake mix over top. Cut butter into small chunks and drop over cake mix. Sprinkle nuts on top and bake 50 to 55 minutes. Serve warm with whipped cream.

Barbara A. Ford   **Cope Middle School, Redlands, CA**

"Punch Bowl" Cake

Serves 6

    1 box chocolate cake mix
    2 (small) packages instant chocolate pudding mix
    1 (16 ounce) Cool Whip
    4 Heath bars, crushed

Bake cake according to package directions in two 8" round cake pans. Let stand overnight or freeze for easier cutting. Slice each layer in half, lengthwise. Prepare pudding according to package directions. In a large punch bowl, layer cake, pudding, Cool Whip and Heath bars; repeat 3 times. Refrigerate until ready to serve. Serve with a spoon.

"A lower calorie version is to use egg whites in the cake, low fat milk in the pudding and fat free Cool Whip. This dessert will always be in center ring!"

Shirley Blough   **Hillside Middle School, Simi Valley, CA**

Raspberry Cake

Serves 12

    1 white cake mix, prepared
    1 (8 ounce) package cream cheese
    1 ½ cups powdered sugar, divided
    1 cup whip cream, whipped
    1 cup raspberries
    1 cup water, divided
    1 cup sugar
    3 tablespoons cornstarch

Prepare white cake mix as package directs; bake, cool and set aside. Mix together cream cheese and 1 cup powdered sugar. In separate bowl, mix 1 cup whipped cream and remaining ½ cup powdered sugar. Fold mixtures together and spread on cooled cake. Simmer raspberries and ⅔ cup water for 3 minutes. Add sugar, cornstarch and remaining ⅓ cup water; bring to a boil; boil 1 minute. Let mixture cool 1 hour, then spread on cake.

"Great tasting on a hot day since it's cool and refreshing."

Ava Smalley   **La Puente High School, La Puente, CA**

Raspberry Mango Shortcakes

Serves 8

Shortcakes:
½ cup coconut
¼ cup sugar
½ teaspoon ginger
1 (17.3 ounce) can Pillsbury Grands! Refrigerated Buttermilk Biscuits
2 tablespoons margarine or butter, melted
Fruit:
2 cups fresh or frozen raspberries, partially thawed
1 ½ cups fresh mangoes, peeled, chopped OR 1 (16 ounce) jar or can mangoes
    or peaches, drained, chopped
2 tablespoons sugar
Topping:
1 cup whipping cream
2 tablespoons brown sugar
¼ teaspoon ginger

Heat oven to 375 degrees. In small bowl, combine coconut, sugar and ginger; blend well. Separate dough into 8 biscuits. Dip top and sides of each biscuit in margarine, dip in coconut mixture. Place biscuits, coconut side up, 2" apart on ungreased cookie sheet. Sprinkle any remaining coconut mixture over tops of biscuits. Bake 14 to 18 minutes or until biscuits and coconut are light golden brown. Cool 5 minutes. Meanwhile, in medium bowl, combine raspberries, mangoes and sugar; stir gently. In small bowl, combine all topping ingredients; beat until stiff peaks form. To serve, split biscuits, place bottom halves on 8 individual plates. Spoon generous ⅓ cup fruit mixture over each biscuit half. Top each with ¼ cup topping and biscuit top. Store in refrigerator.

> *"When I made this for my mother, she said 'Oh, Nancy, don't buy me any more gifts. This is all I need. Just make this for me.'" "Nancy Flesch, Pillsbury 37th Bake Off Contest Cookbook.*

Pillsbury   **Minneapolis, MN**

Raspberry Refrigerator Cake

Serves 10 - 12

¼ pound butter, softened
1 ½ cups powdered sugar
2 eggs
1 box vanilla wafers, chopped up in blender
1 quart raspberries, fresh or frozen, thawed, drained
12 ounces whipped cream

Mix together butter, powdered sugar and eggs, set aside. Layer a 9" x 13" dish accordingly: 1st layer: ⅔ cookie crumbs; 2nd layer: butter mixture; 3rd layer: raspberries; 4th layer: whipped cream; 5th layer ⅓ cookie crumbs. Store in refrigerator until ready to serve.

> *"I had this over at a friend's house, and he got the recipe from his mom...good stuff!"*

Tami Fuhrmann-Cramer   **Kelseyville High School, Kelseyville, CA**

Red Velvet Cake

Serves 10 - 12

Cake:
1 cup oil
1 ½ cups sugar
2 eggs
1 teaspoon vanilla
1 teaspoon vinegar
2 tablespoons cocoa
1 cup buttermilk
1 ounce red food color
2 cups flour
1 teaspoon baking soda
1 teaspoon baking powder
½ teaspoon salt
Cream Cheese Frosting:
8 ounces cream cheese, softened
½ cup butter
2 cups powdered sugar
½ cup walnuts or pecans

Preheat oven to 350 degrees. Cream oil, sugar and eggs. Beat in vanilla, vinegar and cocoa. Beat in buttermilk and food color. Sift flour, soda, baking powder and salt. Add by cups into batter until smooth. Pour into well greased and floured 9" x 13" pan. Bake 25 minutes, or until done. Frosting: Cream butter and cream cheese together. Mix in powdered sugar until smooth. Stir in nuts. Spread on cooled cake.

"Great recipe for Christmas and Valentine's Day."

Alice Claiborne   **Fairfield High School, Fairfield, CA**

Root Beer Cake

Serves 12

1 package Betty Crocker Super Moist white cake mix
1 cup root beer
¼ teaspoon root beer concentrate, if desired
Powdered sugar
Vanilla ice cream
Root beer candies, crushed

Heat oven to 350 degrees. Prepare and bake cake mix in 12 cup bundt cake pan as directed on package - except substitute root beer for the 1 ¼ cups water and add root beer concentrate with root beer. Cool 10 minutes. Invert onto rack of heatproof serving plate; remove pan. Cool cake completely. Sprinkle with powdered sugar. Serve with ice cream sprinkled with candies.

High Altitude Directions (3500 to 6500 feet): Heat oven to 375 degrees. Prepare cake mix as directed in high altitude directions on package except substitute 1 ⅓ cups root beer for the water if using egg whites, or substitute 1 ¼ cups root beer for the water if using whole eggs. Add root beer concentrate with the root beer. Bake 33 to 38 minutes.

General Mills   **Minneapolis, MN**

Soft Centered Chocolate Cakes

Serves 8

¾ cup butter
2 squares unsweetened chocolate
¾ cup chocolate chips
5 eggs, separated
1 ½ tablespoons espresso
1 teaspoon vanilla
⅓ cup sugar
2 tablespoons cocoa
4 tablespoons flour
Dash salt
Powdered sugar

Preheat oven to 375 degrees. In microwave safe dish, melt butter with unsweetened chocolate and chocolate chips. Stir in egg yolks, espresso and vanilla; set aside. In separate bowl, beat egg whites. Add sugar gradually and beat until stiff peaks form. Fold some of the whites into the chocolate mixture. Fold in remaining whites. Sift cocoa, flour and salt and gently fold into chocolate mixture. Divide mixture among 8 buttered custard cups. Place on cookie sheet and bake 10 to 12 minutes (edges should be firm and center soft). Let cool 5 minutes, then invert to serving plates. Sprinkle with powdered sugar.

"Great served with coffee ice cream!"

Cynthia Allen   **Buena High School, Ventura, CA**

Sour Cream Coffee Cake

Serves 10 - 12

Cake:
¼ pound margarine or butter
½ cup shortening
1 ¼ cups sugar
2 eggs
1 teaspoon vanilla
1 small carton sour cream
1 cup flour
1 teaspoon baking powder
½ teaspoon baking soda
Topping:
½ cup nuts
2 tablespoons sugar
½ teaspoon cinnamon

Preheat oven to 350 degrees. Combine cake ingredients and mix well. Pour half of the batter into well greased tube pan. Combine topping ingredients and sprinkle half of the topping over batter. Add remaining batter and top with remaining topping. Bake 1 hour. Sprinkle with powdered sugar while warm.

Kerry Doll   **Fountain Valley High School, Fountain Valley, CA**

Spud & Spice Cake

Serves 8 - 10

1 ¾ cups sugar
1 cup cold mashed potatoes
¾ cup margarine
1 teaspoon cinnamon
½ teaspoon salt
½ teaspoon nutmeg
3 eggs
1 teaspoon baking soda
1 cup sour milk
2 cups + 2 tablespoons flour
¾ cup walnuts (optional)

Preheat oven to 350 degrees. Cream together sugar, mashed potatoes, margarine, cinnamon salt and nutmeg; add eggs. Combine soda and sour milk and stir into creamed mixture. Add flour and walnuts, if using, and blend. Pour into greased and floured loaf pan and bake 50 to 60 minutes.

Sherrie Miles   **Cimarron-Memorial High School, Las Vegas, NV**

Strawberry Cake

Serves 8 - 12

Cake:
1 box frozen strawberries, thawed
½ cup strawberry juice
1 package white cake mix
4 eggs
1 cup oil
½ cup water
1 (13 ounce) package strawberry jello
Icing:
½ stick butter
1 box powdered sugar
½ cup frozen strawberries, thawed

Preheat oven to 350 degrees. Cake: Drain strawberries, reserving ½ cup juice. Combine with remaining cake ingredients and bake 30 to 40 minutes. Icing: combine butter, powdered sugar and strawberries. Punch holes in cake and spread with icing.

Debbie Rothe   **Alta Loma High School, Alta Loma, CA**

Surprise Cupcakes

Makes 24 - 30

1 package chocolate cake mix
⅓ cup sugar
1 (8 ounce) package cream cheese
1 egg
Dash salt
1 (12 ounce) package chocolate chips

Prepare cake mix as directed on package. Fill cupcake liners ⅔ full. Cream together sugar and cream cheese. Beat in egg and salt. Stir in chocolate chips. Drop cream cheese filling by rounded teaspoonfuls into middle of each unbaked cupcake. Bake as directed on cake mix package.

"This was a favorite treat in Jane McPhee's Foods & Nutrition classes before she retired."

Bobbi Witten **Fountain Valley High School, Fountain Valley, CA**

Sweet & Sour Lemon Cake

Serves 12

1 package yellow cake mix
1 package lemon jello
¾ cup oil
¾ cup water
4 eggs
Topping:
2 cups powdered sugar
3 tablespoons lemon juice
1 teaspoon lemon rind, grated

Preheat oven to 350 degrees. Beat first 5 ingredients together for 5 minutes. Pour into a 9" x 13" x 2" pan and bake 35 minutes. Beat topping ingredients together. Poke holes in hot cake with fork. Pour topping over hot cake; cool completely.

"This is a good summer dessert - light and yummy."

Pam Cahill **Eureka High School, Eureka, CA**

Tiramisu

Serves 4

  1 ½ cups nonfat ricotta cheese
  ¼ cup powdered sugar
  ½ teaspoon vanilla extract
  2 cups fresh or frozen strawberries, thawed
  1 tablespoon sugar
  4 slices (½") fat free pound cake
  ¼ cup + 1 teaspoon coffee liqueur
  ½ cup light whipping cream, or whipped topping
  ½ teaspoon cocoa powder

Combine ricotta cheese, powdered sugar and vanilla extract in bowl of a food processor. Process until smooth; set aside. Combine strawberries and sugar in small bowl. Mash together and set aside. Crumble 2 slices pound cake and divide between 4 (10 ounce) balloon wine glasses. In each glass, top cake with 2 tablespoons strawberry mixture, 2 teaspoons coffee liqueur, 3 tablespoons ricotta mixture. Repeat layers. Top each dessert with 2 tablespoons whipped cream and ⅛ teaspoon cocoa powder. Serve immediately.

"This is a popular, dramatic and very tasty recipe."

Judy Henry   **Newhart Middle School, Mission Viejo, CA**

Tortilla Torte

Serves 4

  10 (7 to 8") flour tortillas
  1 (12 ounce) package semi-sweet chocolate pieces
  3 ½ cups dairy sour cream
  ⅓ cup powdered sugar
  Garnish: chocolate curls, fresh strawberries or raspberries, sprig of mint

In a medium saucepan, melt chocolate pieces over low heat, stirring occasionally. Stir in 2 cups of the sour cream. Remove from heat; cool. Place 1 tortilla onto serving plate. Spread about ⅓ cup chocolate mixture atop. Repeat with 8 of the remaining tortillas and remaining chocolate mixture. Top with last tortilla. In a small bowl, stir together the remaining 1 ½ cups sour cream and powdered sugar. Spread on top of torte. Cover and chill overnight. Before serving, wash and dry fruit carefully. Garnish top and around sides of torte with chocolate curls and strawberries or raspberries. Add spring of mint. Slice and serve.

"Very impressive and easy to make."

Kris Hawkins   **Clovis West High School, Clovis, CA**

Triple Chocolate Pudding Cake

Serves 6 - 8

  1 cup biscuit baking mix
  ½ cup sugar
  ¼ cup cocoa
  ¾ cup milk, divided
  ⅓ cup butter, melted
  ¾ cup chocolate topping, divided
  1 teaspoon vanilla
  1 cup chocolate chips, divided
  ¾ cup hot water
  Whipped Topping, if desired

Preheat oven to 350 degrees. Grease an 8" square baking pan. In medium bowl, combine baking mix, sugar and cocoa; stir in ½ cup milk, butter, ¼ cup chocolate topping and vanilla until blended. Stir in ½ cup chocolate chips; spread evenly in prepared pan. In small bowl, combine remaining ¼ cup milk, remaining ½ cup topping and hot water. Pour liquid mixture carefully over top of mixture in pan; do not stir. Sprinkle remaining ½ cup chocolate chips over surface. Bake 40 to 45 minutes or until center is set and cake begins to pull away from sides of pan. Let stand 15 minutes; spoon into dessert dishes, spooning pudding from bottom of pan over top. Serve warm. Garnish with whipped topping, if desired.

Leilani Neiner   **Fontana High School, Fontana, CA**

Vallejo Banana Cake

Serves 10 - 12

- ½ cup milk
- 1 tablespoon vinegar
- 2 cups flour
- 1 teaspoon baking powder
- 1 teaspoon soda
- 1 teaspoon salt
- ½ cup shortening
- 1 ½ cups sugar
- 3 eggs, separated
- 1 teaspoon vanilla
- 1 cup bananas, mashed
- ½ cup walnuts, chopped
- Powdered sugar or prepared buttercream frosting

Preheat oven to 350 degrees. Combine milk and vinegar; set aside. Sift dry ingredients. Cream shortening, sugar, egg yolks and vanilla. Beat egg whites until stiff. Add flour mixture to shortening mixture; mix well. Add bananas and milk; mix well. Fold in egg whites and walnuts. Pour into a greased 9" x 13" pan and bake 35 to 45 minutes. Sprinkle cooled cake with powdered sugar or frost with buttercream frosting.

"I got this recipe from the newspaper. A reader remembered it from her Home Ec. class in Vallejo and sent in a request. Apparently they had quite a number of responses - it is delicious!"

Kathy Warren   **C.K. McClatchy High School, Sacramento, CA**

Vanilla Wafer Cake

Serves 10 - 12

- ½ pound butter
- 2 cups sugar
- 6 eggs
- 12 ounces vanilla wafers, crushed
- ½ cup milk
- 2 (7 ounce) cans coconut, flaked
- 1 cup walnuts

Preheat oven to 275 degrees. Grease and flour angel food cake pan. Cream butter and sugar together. Add eggs, one at a time, beating after each. Add crushed vanilla wafers, milk, coconut and nuts; stir until mixed. Pour into pan and bake 2 ½ hours.

"This takes no frosting. It is like a macaroon cake. Very good warm."

Susan Ballard   **Silverado High School, Victorville, CA**

Yam Cake

Serves 25

- 1 cup butter
- 2 cups sugar
- 4 eggs
- 2 ½ cups sweet potatoes, mashed
- 1 teaspoon vanilla
- 1 teaspoon cinnamon
- ½ teaspoon nutmeg
- 3 cups flour
- 2 teaspoons baking powder
- ½ teaspoon salt
- 1 teaspoon soda
- ½ cup nuts, chopped
- ½ cup coconut

Preheat oven to 325 degrees. Grease a large tube pan and set aside. Cream butter well. Pour sugar in gradually, beating and creaming well. Beat in eggs, one at a time, beating well after each addition. Add mashed potatoes, vanilla and spices. Sift together flour, baking powder, salt and baking soda. Blend into batter. Fold in nuts and coconut. Pour into tube pan and bake 1 hour, 15 minutes.

"Cake is moist and keeps well."

Betty Rabin   **Sierra Vista Junior High School, Canyon Country, CA**

Zona's Wow Cake

Serves 10 - 12

- 1 package yellow cake mix
- 1 large package strawberry banana jello
- 1 cup hot water
- 1 can strawberry soda pop
- 1 small package banana instant pudding
- 1 cup lowfat milk
- 1 small container Cool Whip

Bake cake as package directs in a 9" x 13" pan. Remove from oven, poke holes in cake with a fork. Dissolve strawberry banana jello in hot water and pour over cake. Pour strawberry soda over cake after cake has absorbed jello. Refrigerate 2 hours. Combine instant pudding with milk and Cool Whip. Frost cake and chill until serving.

"Rose Varney shared this with me. She is one of our faithful substitutes and a retired teacher."

Judith Huffman   **Mariposa Co. High School, Mariposa, CA**

Candies

$\mathcal{A}$lmond $\mathcal{J}$oy

Serves 12

2 cups graham cracker crumbs
¼ cup powdered sugar
½ cup butter, melted
1 can sweetened condensed milk
1 cup coconut
1 teaspoon vanilla
1 giant chocolate bar with almonds
1 square baking chocolate

Preheat oven to 350 degrees. Mix cracker crumbs, sugar and melted butter. Pat into bottom of a 9" x 12" pan. Bake for 10 minutes. In a bowl, mix together sweetened condensed milk, coconut and vanilla. Spread over baked crust. Bake 10 minutes. Melt chocolate bar and baking chocolate. Spread over baked coconut, cut and refrigerate.

Debbie Baier   **Poston Junior High School, Mesa, AZ**

$\mathcal{A}$lmond $\mathcal{R}$oca $\mathcal{C}$andy

Serves 12

1 cup butter
1 cup brown sugar
1 cup walnuts, finely chopped
1 (8 ounce) Hershey chocolate bar, broken into pieces

Place butter and brown sugar in a saucepan and bring to a boil; continue to cook, stirring constantly, for 7 minutes. Grease the bottom of a shallow baking dish (9" x 9" x 2") and sprinkle with ½ cup finely chopped walnuts. Pour the butter and sugar mixture over the walnuts and immediately spread with the chocolate pieces. Sprinkle with remaining ½ cup walnuts. Chill in refrigerator to set. Cut into small pieces.

"This recipe was given to me by one of my teaching assistants. It is delicious!"

Elizabeth Ward   **Taft Union High School, Taft, CA**

Butterscotch Peanut Fudge

Makes 4 dozen

1 (12 ounce) package butterscotch pieces
1 (14 ounce) can sweetened condensed milk
1 ½ cups miniature marshmallows
⅔ cup peanut butter, chunk-style
1 teaspoon vanilla
Dash salt
1 cup peanuts, chopped

In saucepan, combine butterscotch pieces, condensed milk and marshmallows. Stir over medium heat until marshmallows melt. Remove from heat; beat in peanut butter, vanilla and dash salt. Stir in nuts. Pour into buttered 9" x 9" x 2" pan. Chill. Cut into squares. Store in refrigerator.

"A tasty departure from the usual chocolate fudge."

Sue Hope   **Lompoc High School, Lompoc, CA**

Candied Walnuts

Makes 2 cups

1 cup sugar
2 teaspoons cinnamon
½ teaspoon ground cloves
¼ teaspoon salt
½ teaspoon nutmeg
¼ cup water
2 cups walnut pieces

Combine sugar, cinnamon, cloves, salt, nutmeg and water in 2 quart saucepan; mix well. Attach candy thermometer. Place on medium heat. Stir mixture constantly until it boils. Continue cooking until mixture reaches soft ball stage 238 degrees on candy thermometer. Remove from heat. Stir in nuts with wooden spoon until syrup coats nuts and become sugary. Spread on waxed paper to cool. Break apart to serve.

"This recipe is a favorite of family and friends. I use it for gift giving."

Judy Herman   **Dublin High School, Dublin, CA**

Caramel Corn-Cracker Jack Style

Serves 8 - 10

- 1 ½ cups popcorn kernels
- 1 ½ cups dry roasted, unsalted peanuts
- *Syrup:*
- 3 cups light brown sugar
- ¾ cup white corn syrup
- 1 ½ cups margarine
- 1 tablespoon salt
- 1 ½ tablespoons baking soda

Using an air popper, pop corn ½ cup at a time. Remove unpopped kernels; stir in nuts. In a heavy saucepan, combine brown sugar, corn syrup, margarine and salt and bring to a boil, then lower heat and simmer 5 minutes; remove from heat and add baking soda. Pour syrup over popcorn and nuts and stir well. Spread coated mixture onto one or two large cookie sheets and bake at 200 degrees, for 1 hour, stirring every 15 minutes. After removing from oven, keep stirring until cool so popcorn won't form into a ball.

"I got this recipe from my wonderful daughter in-law, Shari, and I have prepared this delicious recipe many times! I often add more peanuts than recipe recommends."

Doris L. Oitzman　　　　　　　　　　　　　　**Victor Valley High School, Victorville, CA**

Cashew Brittle

Makes 2 1/2 pounds

- 2 cups sugar
- 1 cup light corn syrup
- ½ cup water
- ½ cup butter or margarine
- 3 cups cashews (about 12 ounces)
- 1 teaspoon baking soda

In heavy 3 quart saucepan combine sugar, corn syrup and water. Cook and stir until sugar dissolves. Bring syrup to boiling; blend in butter or margarine. Stir frequently after mixture reaches the thread stage and candy thermometer registers 230 degrees. Add cashews when temperature reaches soft-crack stage, 280 degrees. Stir constantly until temperature reaches hard-crack stage, 300 degrees. Remove from heat. Quickly stir in baking soda, mixing well. Pour onto 2 buttered 15 ½" x 10 ½" x 1" baking pans. Break into pieces.

"This has turned out to be a real favorite of my family."

Ida Alvey　　　　　　　　　　　　　　**Eldorado High School, Las Vegas, NV**

Christmas Peppermint Creme Crunch

Makes 2 1/2 pounds

- 2 pounds quality white chocolate
- ½ pound red and white candy canes, crushed into small pieces

Melt chocolate over medium heat, stirring until smooth. Remove from heat and stir in crushed peppermint sticks. Pour onto wax paper lined cookie sheet. Chill in refrigerator, about 10 minutes. Break into various size pieces. Store in airtight container.

Carole Call　　　　　　　　　　　　　　**Costa Mesa High School, Costa Mesa, CA**

English Toffee
Makes 1 ½ pounds
1 (2.5 ounce) package almonds, finely chopped
1 cup sugar
2 stick butter
3 tablespoons water
1 teaspoon vanilla
1 cup milk chocolate chips
1 cup walnuts, finely chopped

Line a cookie sheet with aluminum foil; set aside. In a small saucepan, bring almonds, sugar, butter and water to boil, stirring constantly. Cook 9 to 12 minutes more until candy is a rich caramel color. Remove from heat; stir in vanilla. Pour into foil-lined cookie sheet. Sprinkle chocolate chips over top and spread when melted. Top with chopped walnuts and gently press into chocolate. Refrigerate. When cooled completely, break into pieces.
Lisa O'Banion   **Los Banos High School, Los Banos, CA**

Favorite Truffles
Makes 4 dozen
8 ounces cream cheese, softened
4 cups powdered sugar
5 (1 ounce) squares unsweetened chocolate, melted
1 teaspoon vanilla
Cocoa

Beat cream cheese, gradually adding powdered sugar and mixing well after each addition. Add melted chocolate and vanilla; mix well. Chill several hours. Shape into 1" balls. Roll in cocoa. NOTE: Can also be rolled in chopped nuts or powdered sugar. Store in refrigerator.
"A favorite of chocolate loving family members and friends."
Judy Herman   **Dublin High School, Dublin, CA**

Felony Fudge
Makes 24 - 36 pieces
2 cups (12 ounces) peanut butter chips
1 cup semi-sweet chocolate chips
⅓ cup unsalted peanuts, chopped
¼ cup butter or margarine
1 (14 ounce) can sweetened condensed milk

Place all ingredients in a 2 quart microwave-safe bowl. Microwave on 50 percent power 3 to 4 minutes, until all ingredients melt together when stirred; stir until well blended. Pour into an 8" square pan; cover and refrigerate until set. Before cutting into small pieces, let stand at room temperature for 30 minutes.
"This is a reader's favorite from the Orange County Register newspaper."
Bobbi Witten   **Fountain Valley High School, Fountain Valley, CA**

Gigi's Christmas Wreaths

Serves 10 - 12

¼ pound margarine
30 large marshmallows
1 teaspoon green food coloring
1 teaspoon vanilla
3 ½ cups corn flakes
Garnish: green spearmint leaves, red hots

Melt margarine and marshmallows in double boiler. Add food coloring and vanilla. Stir in corn flakes. Quickly form into one big wreath on waxed paper. Garnish with spearmint leaves and red hots for holly berries. Add a big red bow at top

NOTE: You may also form tiny mini-wreaths, about 5" in diameter.

"This recipe comes to me from my grandmother who taught Home Economics for many years. She used this recipe with her students. This makes a great gift. "

Amy Bean   **Cabrillo High School, Lompoc, CA**

Grandma's Fudge

Makes 4 dozen

1 cup margarine
4 cups sugar
1 can evaporated milk
1 (12 ounce) package milk chocolate chips
1 (12 ounce) package semi-sweet chocolate chips
1 (7 ounce) jar marshmallow creme
1 tablespoon vanilla
1 cup nuts, chopped (optional)

Melt margarine in large saucepan. Add sugar and evaporated milk. Bring to a boil; stir constantly for 9 minutes. Remove from heat; add milk chocolate and semi-sweet chocolate chips, marshmallow creme, vanilla and nuts, if desired. Stir well, until mixed. Pour into a greased 9" x 12" pan. Cool completely.

"Delicious, smooth and creamy! Watch carefully so not to burn!"

Donna Small   **Santana High School, Santee, CA**

Jo's Rocky Road Squares

Makes 36

1 (10 ounce) package Ghiradelli milk chocolate squares
1 (6 ounce) package semi-sweet chocolate chips
1 small package miniature marshmallows
⅓ cup walnuts, toasted, chopped

In top of double boiler, melted milk chocolate and chocolate chips together, stirring until smooth. Cool mixture slightly before spreading half of the melted chocolate in a foil-lined squares pan. Sprinkle marshmallows and walnuts evenly on top of mixture. Drop spoonfuls of the remaining chocolate over marshmallow and walnuts. Spread chocolate evenly to cover the marshmallows. Cool before cutting into pieces.

"My husband's grandmother always made theses candies for a special Christmas Eve treat."

Laura de la Motte   **Turlock High School, Turlock, CA**

Microwave Caramel Popcorn

Makes 3 ½ quarts

  4 quarts popped corn (16 cups)
  1 cup brown sugar
  1 stick butter
  ¼ cup white Karo syrup
  ½ teaspoon salt
  ½ teaspoon baking soda

Place popcorn in a large brown grocery bag. Cook at full power for a total of 4 ½ minutes, removing bag and shaking after each 1 ½ minutes cooking time. When done cooking, tear brown bag open and allow to cool. In glass microwave dish with lid (1 ½ quart), combine brown sugar, butter, syrup and salt. Cook at full power for 3 minutes, stirring after each minute. Remove and stir in baking soda. Return to microwave and cook an additional 30 seconds. Pour syrup over popped corn and coat evenly.

"This was shared by my lovely friend, La Vonne Glentzer, a devoted Woodlake FHA parent. It's easy to prepare and the students love it."

Sophia Taylor   **Immanuel High School, Reedley, CA**

Microwave Fudge

Makes 64 pieces

  I cup evaporated milk
  1 tablespoon margarine
  1 ½ cups sugar
  16 marshmallows, cut in half (or equal amount of miniature marshmallows)
  1 (12 ounce) package chocolate chips
  1 cup walnuts, chopped (optional)
  1 teaspoon vanilla

Combine evaporated milk, margarine, sugar and marshmallows in a 2 quart microwave safe bowl. Cook on HIGH 3 to 4 minutes, or until mixture boils; stir. Reduce power to 60% power and microwave another 3 to 4 minutes. Add remaining ingredients. Beat until smooth. Pour into buttered 8" x 8" glass dish. Cool overnight in refrigerator. Cut into 1" squares.

"I got this recipe from English teacher Linda Williamson."

Marilyn Coy   **St. Helena High School, St. Helena, CA**

Old Fashioned Caramels

Makes 48 pieces
- ½ cup butter
- 2 cups sugar
- ¾ cup light corn syrup
- 2 cups whipping cream

In a 2 quart saucepan, bring butter, sugar, corn syrup and one cup whipping cream to a boil, stirring frequently. Slowly add second cup of whipping cream so boiling does not stop. As temperature increases, reduce heat. Cook to 245 degrees on candy thermometer, stirring frequently but careful not to scrape bottom of pan. Watch carefully so mixture does not boil over. When temperature is reached, pour into a well buttered 9" x 13" pan. Let cool overnight. Cut into 1 ½" pieces with buttered knife. Wrap in waxed paper.

"This is my favorite holiday recipe from my Aunt Darb. I used to help her make these at the holidays. They simply melt in your mouth."

Sheri Crouse   **Rhodes Junior High School, Mesa, AZ**

Peanut Butter Bon Bons

Makes 6 dozen
- 1 cup crunchy peanut butter
- ¼ cup butter
- 2 cups powdered sugar
- 1 cup peanuts, ground
- 1 (12 ounce) package chocolate chips
- 1 small (2") piece cocoa butter or paraffin wax

Mix together peanut butter, butter, sugar and peanuts. Roll into small balls. In saucepan, melt chocolate chips and wax over very low heat. Using a toothpick, spear the balls and dip in melted chocolate, coating completely. Place on wax paper to set.

Robin Ali   **Nevada Union High School, Grass Valley, CA**

Quick Almond Brittle

Makes 2 pounds
- 3 cups sugar
- ½ cup butter
- Dash salt
- 1 cup almonds
- 1 (6 ounce) package semi-sweet chocolate morsels
- ½ cup almonds, coarsely chopped

Grease well a 14" x 10" baking pan. Preheat 10" or 12" electric skillet to 400 degrees. Add sugar, butter and salt. When sugar begins to melt, stir to blend. Cook, stirring constantly until sugar dissolves completely, about 3 to 5 minutes. Turn heat control to "OFF". Stir in almonds. Pour into prepared baking pan. Cool slightly. Sprinkle chocolate morsels over candy. Cover baking pan until chocolate morsels are soft. Spread chocolate evenly over candy. Sprinkle chopped almonds over top. Chill until hardened. Break into pieces.

"This is the easiest almond brittle recipe I have ever made. My school principal, Scott McArthur, loves it for Christmas!"

Anita Huckert   **Greenfield Junior High School, Bakersfield, CA**

Serene's Candy Dough

Makes 4 - 6 dozen

Dough:
2 boxes powdered sugar
2 cubes margarine, softened
1 can Eagle brand milk
1 teaspoon vanilla
Additions:
1 cup coconut
1 cup nuts, chopped
Chocolate Topping:
1 (12 ounce) package chocolate chips
⅔ block Parowax

Blend together dough ingredients; divide into 2 parts. To one part, blend in coconut. To second part, blend in chopped nuts. (You may add food coloring at this point if desired.) Chill dough until firm. Roll dough into small balls and chill thoroughly. In top of double boiler, melt chocolate chips slowly with parowax over medium heat. With toothpick, dip each ball into chocolate mixture to coat. Place on cookie sheet and chill.

Marjorie Brown   **Cabrillo High School, Lompoc, CA**

Sherried Pecans

Makes 3 cups

1 ½ cups sugar
½ cup sherry
¼ teaspoon cinnamon
3 cups pecan halves

Cook sugar and sherry to soft ball stage or until candy thermometer reaches 238 degrees. Add cinnamon and quickly stir in pecans. Pour out onto waxed paper and separate into individual pieces.

Judy Dobkins   **Redlands High School, Redlands, CA**

Swedish Nuts

Makes 2 ½ cups

1 cube butter
2 egg whites
Pinch salt
1 cup sugar
1 large can mixed nuts

Preheat oven to 325 degrees. Melt butter in oven on jelly roll pan. Meanwhile, beat egg whites and pinch of salt until stiff. Gradually add sugar and continue beating. When mixed, fold in nuts. Spread onto jelly roll pan evenly. Bake, turning every 10 minutes with a spatula, for a total of 30 minutes. Leave in pan to cool. Remove and break apart.

"A family vacation and holiday favorite for 3 generations. Delicious."

Deanna Potts   **Marina High School, Huntington Beach, CA**

Triple Chocolate Pretzels

Makes 4 dozen

Pretzel Cookie Dough:
2 (1 ounce) squares unsweetened chocolate
½ cup butter or margarine, softened
½ cup sugar
1 egg
2 cups cake flour
1 teaspoon vanilla
¼ teaspoon salt

Mocha Glaze:
1 cup (6 ounce) semi-sweet chocolate chips
1 teaspoon light corn syrup
1 teaspoon shortening
1 cup powdered sugar
3 to 5 tablespoons hot coffee or water

Topping: 2 ounces white chocolate, chopped

Cookie Dough: Melt unsweetened chocolate in top of double boiler over hot, not boiling, water. Remove from heat; cool. Cream butter and sugar in large bowl until light. Add egg and melted chocolate; beat until fluffy. Stir in cake flour, vanilla and salt, until well blended. Cover; refrigerate until firm, about 1 hour. Preheat oven to 400 degrees. Lightly grease cookie sheets or line with parchment paper. Divide dough into 4 equal parts. Divide each part into 12 pieces. To form pretzels, knead each piece briefly to soften dough. Roll into a rope about 6" long. Form into pretzel shape on cookie sheet. Repeat with all pieces of dough, spacing cookies about 2" apart. Bake 7 to 9 minutes, or until firm. Remove to wire racks to cool. Mocha Glaze: Combine chocolate chips, corn syrup and shortening in small heavy saucepan. Stir over low heat until chocolate is melted. Stir in powdered sugar and enough coffee or water to make a smooth glaze. Dip pretzels, one at a time, into glaze to coat completely. Place on waxed paper, right side up. Let stand until glaze is set. Topping: Melt white chocolate in small bowl over hot water. Squeeze melted chocolate through pastry bag over pretzels to decorate. Let stand until chocolate is completely set.

Patti Bartholomew   **Casa Roble High School, Orangevale, CA**

Cheesecakes

Carol's Cheesecake

Serves 12

1 (12 or 13 ounce) can evaporated milk
2 (3 ounce) boxes lemon jello
2 cups boiling water
1 (16 ounce) carton cottage cheese
1 teaspoon vanilla
1 cup sugar
Crust:
1 ½ cups graham cracker crumbs
¼ cup sugar
½ cup butter, melted

Pour evaporated milk into Tupperware container and freeze approximately 3 hours. Dissolve jello in boiling water; set aside to cool. Preheat oven to 350 degrees. Mix crumbs and sugar together. Stir in melted butter. Press firmly into bottom of 9" x 14" pan. Bake 5 minutes; remove to cool. Using an electric mixer, beat together cottage cheese, vanilla and sugar. In small mixer bowl, whip frozen evaporated milk with electric mixer until light and fluffy and resembles whipped cream. Thoroughly mix whipped milk with cottage cheese mixture. Add cooled lemon jello and blend well (color should be creamy pale yellow). Pour into graham cracker crust. Sprinkle with a few graham cracker crumbs. Refrigerate overnight.

"This has been a favorite for years."

Carol Von Berg   **Bear Creek High School, Stockton, CA**

Cherry Cheesecake Pie
Serves 8 - 10

Crust:
1 ¼ cups graham cracker crumbs
2 tablespoons to ¼ cup sugar (to taste)
5 ⅓ tablespoons butter, melted
Filling:
¾ pound cream cheese
½ cup sugar
3 eggs, separated
1 teaspoon pure vanilla extract
⅛ teaspoon almond extract
1 can cherry pie filling

Mix graham cracker crumbs, sugar and melted butter. Pat into pie pan and chill. Blend cream cheese and sugar. Beat until thick and lemon colored. Stir in egg yolks, vanilla and almond extracts. In separate bowl, beat egg whites until soft stiff peaks form, then fold into filling. Pour into chilled crust. Spread with cherry pie filling. Serve chilled.
"An easy dessert! Sure to please!"

Faith Gobuty   **Woodside High School, Woodside, CA**

Chocolate Cheesecake
Serves 8 - 12

Crust:
1 cup flour
1 cube butter, softened
½ cup nuts
Filling:
1 (8 ounce) package cream cheese
1 cup powdered sugar
1 (8 ounce) carton Cool Whip
Topping:
1 box instant chocolate pudding
1 box instant vanilla pudding
3 cups cold milk

Preheat oven to 300 degrees. Crust: Mix together crust ingredients and pat into 9" x 13" pan. Bake 15 minutes; cool. Filling: In mixing bowl, beat together filling ingredients and pour over cooled crust. Topping: Combine pudding mixes with milk and beat until firm. Pour over filling. Refrigerate overnight. Top with whipped cream or Cool Whip.

Variation: You can layer the chocolate and vanilla puddings separately, making a tri-colored dessert. Allow extra time to chill.
"This recipe is a favorite in my hometown of Salina, Utah."

Shauna Wilson   **Cimarron-Memorial High School, Las Vegas, NV**

Chocolate Cheesecake

Serves 6 - 8

Crust:
1 package chocolate wafers
¼ cup sugar
¼ cup butter, melted
Filling:
1 cup whipping cream
1 (8 ounce) package cream cheese, softened
1 (14 ounce) can Eagle brand milk
⅔ cup chocolate syrup
Garnish: chocolate slivers, raspberries

Mix all crust ingredients in a food processor until wafers are fine. Press into a pie dish that has been sprayed with nonstick cooking spray. Whip whipping cream in small mixer bowl until soft peaks are formed; set aside. In large mixer bowl, beat softened cream cheese until fluffy. Add milk and chocolate. Fold in whipped cream on low speed. Pour into chocolate crust and cover with plastic wrap. Freeze 8 hours or overnight. Garnish with slivered chocolate or raspberries and whipped cream.

"Always a favorite!!"

Gail McAuley   **Lincoln High School, Stockton, CA**

Chocolate Swirl Cheesecake

Serves 12

1 ½ cups graham cracker crumbs
3 tablespoons sugar
⅓ cup margarine, melted
24 ounces cream cheese
1 cup sugar
½ teaspoon vanilla
½ teaspoon salt
4 eggs
1 cup chocolate chips, melted

Preheat oven to 325 degrees. Mix graham cracker crumbs, sugar and melted margarine. Press on bottom and sides of a 9" or 10" springform pan. Blend cream cheese and sugar. Add vanilla, salt and eggs; beat well. Pour ½ mixture into crust. Drizzle ½ melted chocolate chips over mixture. Add remaining cream cheese mixture and drizzle remaining chocolate chips on top. Mix with a knife to swirl. Bake 1 hour. Cool 3 hours before serving.

"If desired, serve with 1 tablespoon Hainey's Bristol Cream or Kahlua over top of each slice."

Carol Hagerbaumer   **Chino High School, Chino, CA**

Cookies & Cream Cheesecake

Serves 8 - 10

 2 cups (24) creme filled chocolate cookies, crushed
 6 tablespoons margarine, softened
 1 envelope unflavored gelatin
 ¼ cup cold water
 1 (8 ounce) package Neufchatel cheese, softened
 ½ cup sugar
 ¾ cup nonfat milk
 1 cup whipping cream, whipped
 1 ¼ cups (10) creme filled chocolate cookies, chopped

Combine crushed cookies and margarine; press onto bottom and 1 ½" up sides of 9" springform pan. Soften gelatin in water, stir over low heat until dissolved. Combine Neufchatel cheese and sugar, mixing at medium speed until well blended. Gradually add gelatin and milk, mixing until blended. Chill until mixture is thickened, but not set. Fold in whipped cream. Reserve 1 ½ cups mixture. Pour remaining mixture over crust. Top with chopped cookies and reserved mixture. Chill until firm.

"This cheesecake is delicious! Everyone who eats this asks for the recipe.
One night, four of us finished one off!"

Teresa Hayes   **Buena High School, Ventura, CA**

Easy As Pie Cheesecake

Serves 6 - 8

 2 packages cream cheese, softened
 ½ cup sugar
 2 teaspoons vanilla
 2 eggs
 1 graham cracker crust
 ½ cup fruit, your choice (optional)
 Garnish: fruit and/or syrup

Preheat oven to 350 degrees. Mix cream cheese, sugar and vanilla at medium speed with electric mixer until well blended. Add eggs, one at a time, mixing well after each. Pour cream cheese mixture into crust. Pour fruit on top and push into cream cheese mixture with a knife, making sure fruit is covered. Bake 30 to 35 minutes or until center is set. Cool and top with additional fruit or syrup or serve plain.

"Use fat free cream cheese and add 3/4 cup sugar instead for a lowfat recipe."

Julie Latham   **Alhambra High School, Alhambra, CA**

Mary's Christmas Rum Cheesecake

Serves 12

Crust:
1 ¼ cups graham cracker crumbs
¼ cup sugar
6 tablespoons butter, melted

Rum Filling:
1 envelope unflavored gelatin
1 cup sugar, divided
½ cup light Bacardi rum
1 tablespoon lime peel, grated
½ cup lime juice
4 eggs, separated
2 (8 ounce) packages cream cheese, softened
1 cup (½ pint) heavy cream

Crust: Combine graham cracker crumbs, sugar and melted butter (reserve 3 tablespoons crumb mixture for topping) and press remainder into bottom of 9" springform pan; chill. Filling: Combine gelatin and ½ cup sugar in medium saucepan; stir in rum, lime peel and juice. Beat egg yolks and blend into rum mixture. Cook over medium heat, stirring constantly, until slightly thickened, about 8 minutes; remove from heat. Beat in cream cheese until smooth; set aside. In a bowl, beat egg whites until foamy. Gradually beat in remaining ½ cup sugar, beating until stiff peaks form. In separate bowl, beat heavy cream to soft peaks. Fold egg whites and whipped cream into rum mixture. Turn into crumb crust and sprinkle with reserved crumbs. Cover and chill several hours, or until firm.

Rosemary Garland   **Ontario High School, Ontario, CA**

Peanut Butter Cup Cheesecake

Serves 12

Crust:
8 peanut butter sandwich cookies
⅓ cup dry roasted peanuts
1 teaspoon sugar
1 tablespoon butter

Filling:
3 (8 ounce) packages cream cheese, softened
1 cup sugar
½ cup sour cream
1 tablespoon vanilla
3 large eggs
6 regular size peanut butter cups, chopped

Topping:
¼ cup smooth peanut butter
½ cup sour cream

Garnish: chocolate curls

Preheat oven to 350 degrees. Spray a 9" springform pan with nonstick cooking spray. Crust: In food processor, pulse cookies, peanuts and sugar until finely ground. Add butter, pulse until moistened. Press into bottom of prepared pan. Filling: In large bowl with electric mixer, beat cream cheese 2 to 3 minutes. Gradually beat in sugar, scraping sides of bowl. Add sour cream and vanilla. Beat eggs in one at a time until incorporated. Pour half of filling into prepared crust. Set pan in center of a large roasting pan. Carefully pour enough boiling water into roasting pan to reach halfway up the sides of springform pan. Bake 15 minutes. Remove from oven. Scatter candy evenly over top. Add remaining filling. Return to oven. Bake 45 minutes or until almost set. Topping: Mix peanut butter with sour cream. Bake 10 minutes. Chill 8 hours or overnight. Remove from pan. Garnish with chocolate curls.

"This is best if it's made a day before serving."

DeAnna Olsen   **Cerro Villa Middle School, Villa Park, CA**

Pineapple Cheesecake

Serves 10 - 12

Crust:
18 graham crackers
¼ cup butter, melted
Filling:
1 (8 ounce) package cream cheese
1 (3 ounce) package cream cheese
½ cup sugar
2 eggs, well beaten
1 teaspoon vanilla
1 (26 ounce) can crushed pineapple, drained
Dash cinnamon
Topping:
1 pint sour cream
2 tablespoons sugar
1 teaspoon vanilla

Crust: Roll crackers into fine crumbs and mix with melted butter. Press into 10" pie shell or 9" springform pan. Filling: Cream together cream cheese and sugar. Add eggs and vanilla. Stir in pineapple and dash of cinnamon. Pour over crust and bake at 375 degrees for 20 minutes (or until set in middle). Remove from oven and cool 5 minutes. Increase oven heat to 500 degrees. Topping: Mix sour cream, sugar and vanilla. Pour over cheesecake and bake for 2 minutes; cool. Chill in refrigerator.

"A favorite dessert of my guests. I am often asked to bring this to pot lucks
and special occasions. You'll really enjoy this recipe!"

Amber Bradley   **Granite Hills High School, El Cajon, CA**

Pumpkin Maple Cheesecake

Serves 12

1 ½ cups gingersnap cookie crumbs
¼ cup margarine, melted
3 (8 ounce) packages cream cheese, softened
1 (14 ounce) can sweetened condensed milk
1 (16 ounce) can pumpkin
3 eggs
¾ cup maple syrup
2 teaspoons pumpkin pie spice
Maple Whipped Cream:
1 cup whipping cream
¼ cup maple syrup

Preheat oven to 300 degrees. Combine cookie crumbs and margarine; press into bottom and sides of a 9" springform pan. In large mixer bowl, beat cream cheese until fluffy. Gradually beat in sweetened condensed milk until smooth. Add pumpkin, eggs, syrup and spices; mix well. Pour into prepared pan. Bake 1 hour, 20 minutes. Turn off oven and allow cheesecake to cool in oven with door slightly open. Remove from oven and chill in refrigerator. Beat whipping cream with maple syrup. Garnish cheesecake with maple whipped cream.

"For Thanksgiving dinner dessert change, this is fun to serve instead of traditional pumpkin pie."
Carol Hagerbaumer   **Chino High School, Chino, CA**

"Worth the Calories" Classic Cheesecake

Serves 16

Crust:
1 ¾ cup graham cracker crumbs (about 15 crackers)
¼ cup walnuts, finely chopped (optional)
½ teaspoon cinnamon
⅓ cup butter, melted
Filling:
3 eggs, well beaten
2 (8 ounce) packages cream cheese, softened
1 cup sugar
¼ teaspoon salt
2 teaspoons vanilla
½ teaspoon almond extract
3 cups sour cream

Preheat oven to 375 degrees. Thoroughly mix crust ingredients. Press onto bottom and sides of a 9" springform pan. Sides should be almost 1 ¾" high. Combine eggs, cream cheese, sugar, salt, vanilla and almond extract; beat until smooth. Blend in sour cream. Do not over-mix (too much air causes cracks). Pour into crumb crust and bake 35 minutes or until just set. Chill thoroughly, about 4 or 5 hours. Filling will be soft. Best made the day before.

"I got this recipe from a woman (fellow student) in my first Home Economics cooking class at Mt. SAC in 1963. I've tried many other recipes, but none compare. My 8th graders make this is in class. They are very successful and proud. Slice thin, it's very rich."

Carol Steele   **LaPaz Intermediate School, Mission Viejo, CA**

Cookies

Apple Bars

Makes 2 dozen

2 ½ cups flour
2 teaspoons sugar
½ teaspoon salt
1 cup shortening
⅔ cup milk
2 egg yolks (reserve whites)
6 Granny Smith apples
1 ½ cups sugar
1 teaspoon cinnamon
Glaze:
1 cup powdered sugar
1 tablespoon (or more) milk
½ teaspoon almond extract

Preheat oven to 400 degrees. Mix together dry ingredients and cut in shortening. Beat milk and egg yolks together, then mix with dry ingredients. Divide dough into 2 parts; roll each between waxed paper to approximately 9" x 13". Press 1 part of dough into bottom of ungreased 9" x 13" glass pan. Peel and slice apples. Sprinkle with sugar and cinnamon and toss to coat. Pour apples over pastry. Cover with remaining half of dough, pressing into corners and sides. Brush with egg white and bake 35 to 40 minutes. Combine powdered sugar with enough milk to make a thin glaze, stir in almond extract. When apple bars are cooled, drizzle with glaze.

"Better than any apple pie!!!"

Charlotte Heitzmann   **Mariposa Co. High School, Mariposa, CA**

Banana Treats

Serves 4
 2 bananas
 ½ cup cream cheese
 ½ cup walnuts halves

Slice bananas in crosswise rings, about ½" thick. Put a dollop, about 1 teaspoon cream cheese on top of each slice. Place a walnut half on top of cream cheese.

"These are even good for a snack - not really sweet."

Jane Souza **North Monterey Co. High School, Castroville, CA**

Berry Luscious

Serves 12
 Fruit Filling:
 1 (16 ounce) package frozen blackberries
 ½ cup sugar
 ¼ cup water
 3 tablespoons cornstarch
 Crust:
 1 ½ cups flour
 1 cup butter or margarine
 ½ cup walnuts, chopped
 Cream cheese filling:
 1 cup powdered sugar
 8 to 12 ounces cream cheese

Preheat oven to 350 degrees. Fruit filling: Mix blackberries, sugar, water and cornstarch in a medium saucepan; bring to a boil, turn down heat and simmer 3 minutes. Set aside to cool. Crust: Mix together butter, flour and nuts. Press into a 9" x 13" pan. Bake 15 minutes. Let cool. Cream Cheese Filling: Mix powdered sugar and cream cheese until fluffy. Spread on baked crust. Pour blackberry filling over cream cheese and chill. Serve with vanilla ice cream or whipped cream.

"A refreshing summer treat!"

Maria Montemagni **Strathmore High School, Strathmore, CA**

Best Oatmeal Cookies

Makes 5 dozen
 2 cups margarine or butter
 1 ½ cups sugar
 1 ½ cups brown sugar
 4 eggs
 2 teaspoons vanilla
 2 ½ cups all-purpose flour
 2 cups whole wheat flour
 2 teaspoons baking powder
 2 teaspoons baking soda
 2 cups oatmeal
 3 cups raisin bran or other flaked cereal

1 ½ cups M&M candies or baking chips
1 ½ cups chocolate chips
1 cup nuts, chopped (optional)
1 cup shredded coconut (optional)

Preheat oven to 350 degrees. In large mixing bowl, cream together margarine or butter, sugars, eggs and vanilla. In separate bowl, combine flours, baking powder and soda. Beat dry ingredients slowly into creamed mixture until well combined. Stir in oatmeal, cereal, candies, chocolate chips and nuts and coconut, if desired. Drop onto cookie sheet and bake 10 to 15 minutes, to desired doneness.

"I like the flavor the whole wheat flour gives the cookie. I use any corn flake or bran flake cereal as we get to the bottom of the box to use up the small flakes and get rid of the cereal."
Jeanette Atkinson   **Brinley Middle School, Las Vegas, NV**

Black Walnut Brownies

Makes 30 bars
1 ¼ cups butter or margarine
¾ cup cocoa
2 cups sugar
4 eggs
1 tablespoon vanilla
1 ¼ cups flour
½ teaspoon salt
⅛ teaspoon baking powder
1 cup black walnuts, chopped

Preheat oven to 350 degrees. In a large bowl, combine butter or margarine, cocoa, sugar, eggs, and vanilla; blend well. In a separate bowl, sift together flour, salt and baking powder. Add to cocoa mixture and stir until smooth. Add nuts. Pour batter into a greased and floured 15 ½" x 10 ½" jelly roll pan and spread evenly. Bake 25 minutes. Cool before cutting into bars.

"Regular walnuts may be substituted for black walnuts."
Pat Grow   **Moapa Valley High School, Overton, NV**

Blondies

Serves 8
2 cups graham cracker crumbs
1 (6 ounce) package chocolate chips
1 can fat free Eagle brand milk

Preheat oven to 350 degrees. Combine all ingredients and press into an 8" x 8" pan. Bake 20 minutes. Cool completely before cutting.

"This is to die for and so easy! All you need is a large glass of milk with it."
Vicki Giannetti   **Foothill High School, Sacramento, CA**

Boston Cremes

Makes 5 dozen

2 cups sugar
1 cup shortening
¾ cup dark molasses
2 eggs
1 teaspoon salt
1 teaspoon cloves
2 teaspoons cinnamon
1 tablespoon baking soda
¾ cup hot water
4 ½ cups flour

Cream together sugar and shortening. Add molasses, eggs, salt and spices. Dissolve baking soda in hot water and stir into batter. Slowly add flour to make soft dough. Chill dough. When ready to bake, preheat oven to 450 degrees. Roll out dough and cut into shapes. Bake 5 to 10 minutes, until desired doneness.

"This has been passed down for about 60 years. The recipe makes wonderful gingerbread men during the holidays. I frost with royal icing (white) and then, using a sponge and colored royal icing - splatter."

Jeri Lundy   **Grossmont High School, La Mesa, CA**

Bowknots

Makes 6 - 7 dozen

6 eggs
3 tablespoons sugar
¼ teaspoon salt
½ teaspoon orange extract
1 teaspoon almond extract
3 cups flour
2 tablespoons butter
3 cups peanut oil
½ cup powdered sugar

Beat eggs lightly. Add sugar, salt and flavorings; blend thoroughly. Place flour in a bowl and cut in butter. Add egg mixture and form a ball. Knead until smooth. If dough is too soft, add more flour to make it firm, but not hard. Set aside for 30 minutes. Cut dough into 4 sections. Roll each section, one at a time, on a floured board until wafer thin; cut into strips 6" long by ¾" wide. Tie in individual bowknots. Heat peanut oil in deep fryer. Fry bows about 3 minutes or until golden brown. Drain on absorbent paper; cool. Sprinkle with powdered sugar.

Angela Croce   **Mira Mesa High School, San Diego, CA**

Butter Nut Chewies

Makes 2 dozen

> 2 eggs
> 2 cups brown sugar, finely packed
> 1 teaspoon vanilla
> ½ cup margarine, melted
> 1 ½ cups unsifted flour
> 2 teaspoons baking powder
> ½ teaspoon salt
> 1 cup nuts, finely chopped

Preheat oven to 350 degrees. Grease a 13" x 9" x 2" pan. Beat eggs until light and foamy in large bowl of electric mixer. Beat in sugar, vanilla and melted margarine until creamy and soft. Combine flour with baking powder and salt. Add to egg mixture. Mix at low speed until blended. Stir in nuts at low speed (mixture will be stiff). Spread evenly in prepared pan. Bake 25 to 30 minutes or until top is light brown. Cool 10 to 15 minutes; cut into bars.

"My sister-in-law's yummy recipe."

Carmen Leonard　　　　　　　　　　**Mission Viejo High School, Mission Viejo, CA**

Butterfinger Morsel Brownies

Serves 12

> 1 box brownie mix, prepared according to package directions
> 2 extra large Butterfinger candy bars
> 1 cup chocolate morsels

Prepare brownies according to package directions. While they bake, crumble candy bars. When brownies are done, remove from oven and immediately sprinkle with crumbled candy bars and chocolate morsels. The heat from the brownies will melt topping. Leave as is, or spread with a spatula for a smoother top.

"Add walnuts, peanuts, almonds, pecans or cashews to mix or frosting layer."

Susan Ulrich　　　　　　　　　　**Savanna High School, Anaheim, CA**

Butterscotch Bars

Makes 24 to 30

> ½ cup butter, melted
> 2 cups brown sugar, packed
> 2 eggs
> 2 cups sifted flour
> 2 teaspoons baking powder
> ½ teaspoon salt
> ½ cup nuts, chopped
> 2 teaspoons vanilla
> Powdered sugar, for dusting on top

Preheat oven to 325 degrees. Add butter to sugar and cool; blend in eggs. Stir in remaining ingredients. Spread in 13" x 9" baking pan. Bake about 30 minutes. While still warm, cut into bars. Dust with powdered sugar, if desired.

Pam Ford　　　　　　　　　　**Temecula Valley High School, Temecula, CA**

Candy Cane Cookies

Makes 3 dozen
>1 cup shortening
>1 cup powdered sugar, sifted
>1 egg
>1 ½ teaspoons vanilla
>1 ½ teaspoons almond extract
>2 ½ cups flour
>1 teaspoon salt
>Red food color
>½ cup peppermint candy, crushed
>½ cup sugar

Preheat oven to 350 degrees. Cream shortening and powdered sugar in large mixing bowl. Add egg and flavorings, beating until fluffy. Stir in flour and salt; mix well. Divide dough in half. Add a few drops of red food color to half of dough still in large mixing bowl. Stir until red color is uniform. Roll 1 tablespoon of dough of each color into long strip. Twist white and red dough strips together. Place on cookie sheet. Bake 10 minutes. Crush peppermint candy in ziploc bag with sugar. While cookies are warm, sprinkle with peppermint sugar.

"This recipe is my fiancee's favorite holiday cookie."

Kristine Hubbard   **San Luis Obispo High School**
                                                       San Luis Obispo, CA

Caramel Brownies

Makes 20 - 25
Brownies:
>4 eggs, beaten
>2 ¼ cups brown sugar
>2 cups flour
>1 teaspoon cinnamon
>1 teaspoon salt
>1 cup pecans, chopped
Frosting:
>1 pound powdered sugar
>1 (8 ounce) package cream cheese, softened
>1 cube margarine, softened
>1 teaspoon vanilla

Preheat oven to 350 degrees. Mix brownie ingredients in a large bowl. Spread into a greased jelly roll pan (batter will be very thick). Bake 15 to 20 minutes; cool. Whip frosting ingredients together. Spread on cooled brownies. Cut into squares and serve.

"These are absolutely delicious!!! The recipe seems odd because there is no fat and no leavening in the brownies, but the eggs serve as the fat and leavening."

Kathy Sandoz   **Mesa Junior High School, Mesa, AZ**

Tasty Fruit Desserts

Raspberry Mango Shortcakes, page 35

Fruit Tacos

page 101

*Carmel and Chocolate-
Great Combo!*
Chocolate-Caramel-Pecan Squares
page 17

Caramel Layer Chocolate Squares

Makes 36 squares

50 light caramels (14 ounce package)
⅔ cup evaporated milk, divided
1 package German chocolate cake mix
½ cup margarine, melted
1 cup nuts, chopped
1 cup chocolate chips

Preheat oven to 350 degrees. In saucepan, combine caramels and ⅓ cup evaporated milk. Cook over low heat, stirring constantly until thoroughly blended; set aside. Grease and flour a 9" x 13" pan. In mixing bowl, combine cake mix with butter, ⅓ cup evaporated milk and nuts. By hand, stir dough until it holds together. Press ½ dough into prepared pan. Bake 6 minutes. Sprinkle chips over crust. Spread caramel mix over chocolate chips. Crumble reserved dough over caramel and return to oven. Bake 15 to 18 minutes. Cool slightly, then refrigerate 30 minutes to set caramel layer and cut into 36 squares.

Donna Swennes **El Capitan High School, Lakeside, CA**

Carrot Cookies

Makes 24

¾ cup sugar or honey
¾ cup butter
1 egg
1 cup carrots, cooked and mashed
2 cups flour
2 teaspoons baking powder
½ teaspoons salt
1 teaspoon vanilla
½ cup walnuts, chopped
Icing:
½ package powdered sugar
1 tablespoon grated orange peel
orange juice

Preheat oven to 375 degrees. Mix sugar or honey, butter, egg and carrots together. Stir in flour, baking powder, salt and vanilla. Fold in walnuts. Drop dough onto greased cookie sheets by teaspoonfuls. Bake 12 minutes. Icing: Mix together powdered sugar, orange peel and just enough orange juice to make icing desired consistency. When cooled, frost with orange icing.

"These are my family's favorites."

Katrina Brighton **Swainston Middle School, Las Vegas, NV**

Cathedral Windows

Makes 6 - 8 dozen
> 1 (12 ounce) package mini Nestlé's semi-sweet chocolate pieces
> 1 stick margarine
> 1 cup nuts, chopped
> 1 package colored miniature marshmallows
> 1 can coconut

Melt mini chocolate pieces with butter; cool. Add nuts and marshmallows. Form into two logs on 14" x 18" pieces of waxed paper. Roll logs in coconut; roll up in waxed paper and refrigerate overnight. Slice into ½" pieces.

"These are very easy, very attractive and very good!"

Gage Hewes　　　　　　　　　　　**South Pasadena High School, South Pasadena, CA**

Cheesecake Brownies

Makes 24
> 1 (21.5 ounce) box brownie mix
> 1 (8 ounce) package cream cheese, softened
> ⅓ cup sugar
> 1 egg
> ½ teaspoon vanilla

Preheat oven to 350 degrees. Prepare brownie mix as directed on package, using a greased 13" x 9" baking pan. Pour batter into pan and set aside. Beat cream cheese with electric mixer on medium speed until smooth. Add sugar, mixing until blended. Add egg and vanilla; mix just until blended. Pour cream cheese mixture over brownie batter; cut though batter with knife several times for marbled effect. Bake 35 to 40 minutes.

Shirley Marshman　　　　　　　　　　**West Middle School, Downey, CA**

Chewy Chocolate Cookies

Makes 4 ½ dozen
> 1 ¼ cups butter or margarine, softened
> 2 cups sugar
> 2 eggs
> 2 teaspoons vanilla
> 2 cups unsifted all-purpose flour
> ¾ cup Hershey's cocoa
> 1 teaspoon baking soda
> ½ teaspoon salt
> 1 cup nuts, finely chopped (optional)

Preheat oven to 350 degrees. Cream butter or margarine and sugar in large mixer bowl. Add eggs and vanilla; blend well. Combine flour, cocoa, baking soda and salt; blend into creamed mixture. Stir in nuts, if desired. Drop by teaspoonfuls onto ungreased cookie sheet. Bake 8 to 9 minutes. (DO NOT OVERBAKE. Cookies will be soft. They will puff during baking and flatten upon cooling). Cool on cookie sheet until set, about 1 minute; remove to wire rack to cool completely.

"This is a real crowd pleasing cookie!!"

Linda Woolley　　　　　　　　　　**Redlands East Valley High School, Redlands, CA**

Chocolate Caramel Twix Bars

Makes 24 bars

Crust:
½ cup + 2 tablespoons butter (not margarine)
¼ cup sugar
1 ¼ cups flour
Filling:
½ cup butter
½ cup brown sugar
2 tablespoons corn syrup
½ cup sweetened condensed milk
Topping:
½ cup chocolate
1 tablespoon butter

Preheat oven to 375 degrees. Crust: Cream butter, sugar and flour and press into an 8" square pan. Bake 20 to 25 minutes. Filling: In saucepan, combine filling ingredients and bring to a boil over low heat. Boil 5 minutes, stirring constantly. Remove from heat and pour over baked crust. Topping: In saucepan, melt topping ingredients over low heat, then pour over cooled caramel layer. Allow to cool and cut into small pieces.

Anita Cornwall   **Cimarron Memorial High School, Las Vegas, NV**

Chocolate Chip Brownies

Makes 32

1 ½ cups flour
1 teaspoon baking powder
1 teaspoon salt
2 cups sugar
1 cup oil
4 eggs
2 teaspoon vanilla
4 envelopes unsweetened chocolate, melted
1 (12 ounce) package semi-sweet chocolate chips
Powdered sugar

Preheat oven to 350 degrees. Sift flour, baking powder and salt into a bowl. Add sugar and mix into sifted ingredients. Make a well in center and add oil and eggs. Add vanilla and melted unsweetened chocolate and beat until smooth. Stir in chocolate chips, Pour into greased pan and bake for 30 to 35 minutes. Let cool 15 to 20 minutes before cutting. Sprinkle lightly with powdered sugar.

"Absolutely delicious...my family loves them!!!"

Melissa Webb   **Lakewood High School, Lakewood, CA**

Chocolate Chip, Oats'n Caramel Cookie Squares

Makes 16

1 (18 ounce) package Pillsbury Refrigerated Chocolate Chip Cookies
1 cup quick-cooking rolled oats
Dash salt, if desired
5 tablespoons Pillsbury BEST all Purpose Flour
⅔ cup caramel ice cream topping
1 teaspoon vanilla
¾ cup walnuts, chopped
1 (6 ounce) package (1 cup) semi-sweet chocolate chips

Preheat oven to 350 degrees. In large bowl, break up cookie dough with wooden spoon. Add oats and salt; mix until well blended. Reserve ½ cup cookie dough mixture; press remaining mixture in ungreased 9" square pan. Bake 10 to 12 minutes or until cookie dough puffs and appears dry. In small bowl, combine flour, caramel topping and vanilla; blend well. Sprinkle walnuts and chocolate chips evenly over partially baked crust. Drizzle evenly with caramel mixture. Crumble reserved ½ cup cookie dough mixture over caramel. Bake an additional 20 to 25 minutes or until golden brown. Cool 10 minutes. Run knife around sides of pan to loosen. Cool 1 ½ hours or until completely cooled. Cut into bars.

Pillsbury   **Minneapolis, MN**

Chocolate Chip Pumpkin Cookies

Makes 6 - 8 dozen

1 cup oil
2 eggs
4 cups sugar
4 cups pumpkin
5 cups flour
1 teaspoon cinnamon
½ teaspoon nutmeg
4 teaspoons baking soda
1 teaspoon cloves
2 cup pecans or almonds, chopped
1 cup granola, oatmeal or grape nuts cereal
1 (12 ounce) package chocolate chips

Preheat oven to 375 degrees. Combine and blend oil, eggs, sugar and pumpkin. In another bowl, sift together dry ingredients; blend into wet ingredients. Stir in nuts, cereal and chocolate chips. Drop on greased cookie sheet and bake 10 to 12 minutes.

"Use a very large bowl. You'll need it!"

Joan Goodell   **Eldorado High School, Las Vegas, NV**

Chocolate, Chocolate, Chocolate Chip Cake

Serves 12

1 package devil's food chocolate cake mix
1 small box instant chocolate pudding mix
1 (8 ounce) carton sour cream
4 eggs
½ cup water
½ cup vegetable oil
1 (12 ounce) package chocolate chips

Preheat oven to 350 degrees. In large mixing bowl, combine cake mix, pudding mix, sour cream, eggs, water and oil; beat until well blended, about 2 minutes. Stir in chocolate chips. Pour batter into a greased bundt pan or greased 13" x 9" x 2" pan. Bake 1 hour. Remove from oven; cool. Sprinkle with powdered sugar.

"My sister, Jan Cottrell, gave this recipe to me. It is very moist and is great with vanilla ice cream."

Tricia Montelongo   **South Junior High School, Anaheim, CA**

Chocolate Crinkles

Makes 4 dozen

½ cup oil
4 squares unsweetened chocolate, melted
2 cups sugar
4 eggs
2 teaspoons vanilla
2 cups flour
2 teaspoons baking powder
½ teaspoon salt
1 cup powdered sugar

Mix oil, melted chocolate and sugar; blend in eggs one at a time until well mixed. Add vanilla. Stir in flour, baking powder and salt. Chill several hours or overnight. Heat oven to 350 degrees. Roll dough into balls and drop in powdered sugar. Place on greased baking sheet and bake 10 to 12 minutes.

"These satisfy anyone's chocolate cravings!"

Maria Montemagni   **Strathmore High School, Strathmore, CA**

Chocolate Decadence Brownies

Makes 40

Brownies:
4 ounces unsweetened chocolate
1 cup butter
4 eggs
2 cups sugar
1 tablespoon vanilla
¼ teaspoon salt
1 cup flour
Frosting:
4 ounces unsweetened chocolate
1 cup butter
2 eggs
1 tablespoon vanilla
1 pound powdered sugar
4 cups miniature marshmallows

Preheat oven to 350 degrees. In a large saucepan, combine chocolate and butter. Heat over low heat until melted and smooth, stirring occasionally. Remove from heat and beat in eggs, sugar, vanilla and salt until thoroughly blended. Stir in flour. Spread evenly in bottom of greased 9" x 13" baking pan. Bake 25 to 30 minutes. Brownies should be moist. Do not over-bake. Cool in pan. Frosting: In a medium saucepan, combine chocolate and butter; heat over low heat until melted and smooth, stirring occasionally. Remove from heat and add eggs, vanilla and powdered sugar. Beat until smooth. Stir in marshmallows. While frosting is slightly warm, spread over brownies. Refrigerate several hours or overnight. Cut chilled brownies into 1 ½" squares. Store in refrigerator.

> *"These are very, very rich!! They are a favorite when featured on the menu at our Golden Eagle Cafe."*

Donna Hamilton   **Del Oro High School, Loomis, CA**

Chocolate Marshmallow Bars

Makes 46 bars

1 cup butter or margarine
2 cups sugar
1 teaspoon vanilla
4 eggs
1 ¾ cups flour
½ cup cocoa
1 cup nuts, chopped
1 cup coconut, flaked
1 (7 ounce) jar marshmallow creme
Cocoa frosting:
½ cup butter or margarine
½ cup cocoa
2 ⅔ cup powdered sugar
1 teaspoon vanilla
6 tablespoons milk

Preheat oven to 350 degrees. Cream butter or margarine, sugar and vanilla in large mixer bowl until light and fluffy. Add eggs; beat well. Combine flour and cocoa; add to creamed mixture, blending well. Stir in nuts and coconut. Spread mixture in greased 15 ½" x 10 ⅓" x 1" jelly roll pan. Bake 30 to 35 minutes. Remove from oven, spoon marshmallow creme over top. Let stand 5 minutes. Carefully spread creme to cover entire surface. Cocoa Frosting: Melt butter over low heat. Add cocoa; heat, stirring constantly until mixture thickens. Do not boil. Remove from heat, pour into small mixer bowl. Add powdered sugar and vanilla. Blend in milk. Beat to spreading consistency. Additional milk may be added. Spread cocoa frosting over bars while slightly warm.

Gale Hooper   **Casa Roble High School, Orangevale, CA**

Chocolate Pixies

Makes 3 dozen
> 2 cups flour, sifted
> 2 teaspoons baking powder
> ½ teaspoon salt
> ¼ cup butter
> 4 (1 ounce) squares baking chocolate
> 2 cups sugar
> 4 eggs
> ½ cup walnuts
> Powdered sugar

Preheat oven to 300 degrees. Sift together flour, baking powder and salt; set aside. Melt butter and chocolate together; remove from heat. Cool slightly. Blend sugar into butter mixture. Add eggs, one at a time. Beat 1 minute. Add flour mixture and walnuts; mix thoroughly; chill at least 15 minutes. Shape into balls using 1 tablespoon dough. Roll in powdered sugar (dip tops a second time). Place on greased cookie sheet and bake 18 to 20 minutes.

"These are always hits. My children's favorites! A chocolate lovers dream."

Carol Fleming   **Rancho Cucamonga High School**
                                                     Rancho Cucamonga, CA

Chunky Hazelnut Toffee Cookies

Makes 4 -½ dozen
> 1 cup unsalted butter, softened
> ¾ cup brown sugar, firmly packed
> ½ cup sugar
> 2 large eggs
> 1 tablespoon vanilla
> 2 ¾ cups flour
> 1 ½ teaspoons baking powder
> ½ teaspoon baking soda
> ½ teaspoon salt
> 4 (1.4 ounce) English toffee candy bars, chopped
> 2 (10 ounce) packages semi-sweet chocolate chunks
> 1 cup hazelnuts or pecans, toasted, chopped

Preheat oven to 350 degrees. Beat butter at medium speed with electric mixer until creamy. Gradually add sugar, beating well. Add eggs and vanilla; beat well. In another bowl, combine flour, baking powder, soda and salt. Gradually add to butter mixture, beating at low speed just until blended. Stir in toffee candy, chocolate chunks and nuts. Drop dough by heaping table-spoonfuls 1 ½" apart onto ungreased baking sheets. Bake 10 minutes, until golden brown. Cool slightly on baking sheets; remove to wire rack to cool completely.

> *"From Forrest Gump's My Favorite Chocolate Recipes, published by Oxmoore House. I won the chocolate chip cookie contest at school two years in a row with this recipe!"*

Donna Long   **South Hills High School, Covina, CA**

Cookie Clusters

Makes 4 - 5 dozen
1 (12 ounces) package white chocolate chips
2 tablespoons peanut butter
1 ¼ cups Rice Krispies
1 cup Spanish peanuts
1 cup miniature marshmallows

Melt chocolate chips with peanut butter in microwave (refer to package for melting directions); stir and let cool slightly. Stir in cereal and peanuts. Fold in marshmallows. Drop by teaspoonfuls onto waxed paper. Allow to cool at room temperature for at least 20 to 30 minutes before serving. These will keep up to 2 weeks in refrigerator.

> *"You might want to add some fun and color by sprinkling on a little shredded coconut, colored sprinkles or chopped Heath candy bars before cooling."*

Millie Deeton   **Ayala High School, Chino Hills, CA**

Cookies In A Snap

Makes 2 dozen
1 box cake mix, any flavor
½ cup vegetable oil
2 eggs

Preheat oven to 350 degrees. Combine cake mix with oil and eggs. Mix until dough forms. Drop by teaspoonfuls onto cookie sheet approximately 2" apart. Bake 6 to 9 minutes.

NOTE: You may substitute ¼ cup oil + ¼ cup water for ½ cup oil to reduce fat in recipe.

> *"These cookies can be any flavor with a variety of goodies: cherry chip cake with chocolate chips, white cake with coconut, chocolate cake with chocolate chips and walnuts. Make up your own! Have fun!"*

Teresa Stahl   **Needles High School, Needles, CA**

Cranberry Macadamia Bars

Makes 48

Crust:
1 ¼ cups flour
¾ cup sugar
½ cup butter
1 cup macadamia nuts, hazelnuts or pecans, finely chopped, divided

Topping:
1 ¼ cups sugar
2 eggs, beaten
2 tablespoons milk
1 teaspoon orange peel, finely shredded
1 teaspoon vanilla
1 cup cranberries, finely chopped
½ cup coconut

Preheat oven to 350 degrees. Crust: In medium mixing bowl, stir together flour and sugar. Cut in butter until mixture resembles coarse crumbs. Stir in ½ cup nuts. Press into bottom of an ungreased 13" x 9" x 2" pan and bake 10 to 15 minutes, or until crust is light brown around edges. Topping: Combine sugar, eggs, milk, orange peel and vanilla. Beat until combined. Pour over hot crust. Sprinkle with remaining nuts, cranberries and coconut. Bake 30 minutes more or until golden. Cool slightly in pan on wire rack. Cut into 24 bars, then in half diagonally while warm. Cool completely.

"This recipe was given to me by Sets Miyada, our grocery shopper for the past several years. She found it in a Better Homes & Gardens magazine and found it a big hit with her family."

Pat Dallas   **Westminster High School, Westminster, CA**

Famous Oatmeal Chocolate Chip Cookies

Makes 4 dozen
4 cups flour
2 teaspoons vanilla
2 teaspoons baking soda
2 teaspoons salt
2 cups butter
1 cup white sugar
2 cups brown sugar
2 tablespoons water
4 eggs
4 cups oatmeal
2 cups semi-sweet chocolate chips OR 3 cups milk chocolate chips

Preheat oven to 350 degrees. Mix all ingredients in large mixing bowl using paddle beater. If a paddle beater is not available, then mix by hand. Do not whip ingredients - batter must be heavy. Portion cookies onto ungreased cookie sheet using a #40 disher or shape into 2" balls. Bake 8 to 10 minutes. Do not overbake. Allow to cool on cookie sheets.

"These are our famous deli cookies. Use a large ice cream disher for excellent mega cookies - great for kid's lunchbox or fundraiser!!"

DeLisa Davis   **Sutter High School, Sutter, CA**
Kristin Stipanov   **Cabrillo High School, Lompoc, CA**

Finnish Ribbon Cookies

Makes 4 dozen
1 cup butter or margarine, softened
½ cup sugar
1 egg yolk
1 teaspoon vanilla
½ teaspoon grated lemon peel (optional)
2 ½ cups all-purpose flour
¼ teaspoon salt
6 tablespoons berry or apricot jam
½ cup powdered sugar
1 tablespoon milk

Preheat oven to 375 degrees. In large bowl, beat butter and sugar until creamy. Beat in egg yolk, vanilla and lemon peel, if desired. In another bowl, stir together flour and salt. Gradually add to butter mixture, blending thoroughly. Shape dough into 3 or 4 ropes, about ¾" in diameter and as long as your baking sheets. Place them about 2" apart on ungreased baking sheet. With the side of your little finger, press a long groove down the center of each rope (don't press all the way through). Bake cookies 10 minutes. Remove from oven and spoon jam into grooves. Return to oven for 5 to 10 minutes, or until cookies are firm to touch and lightly golden brown. Mix together powdered sugar and milk to make thin glaze. While cookies are warm, drizzle them with powdered sugar glaze mixture. Cut at 45 degree angle into 1" lengths. Let cool briefly on baking sheets. Transfer to racks to cool completely. Store in airtight container.

Adrienne Bahn   **Lee Junior High School, Woodland, CA**

Fudgy Brownies
Serves 24
1 package Duncan Hines Fudge Brownie Mix
2 eggs
⅓ cup water
⅓ cup vegetable oil
¾ cup semi-sweet chocolate chips
½ cup walnuts or pecans, chopped

Preheat oven to 350 degrees. Grease bottom of 13" x 9" pan. Combine brownie mix, eggs, water and oil in large bowl. Stir about 50 strokes with spoon until well blended. Stir in chocolate chips. Spread in pan. Sprinkle nuts on top. Bake 25 to 30 minutes. Do NOT overbake. Cool. Cut into squares.
"These brownies are chewy and delicious. They will satisfy the cravings of any chocoholic."
Myra Skidmore   **Downey High School, Downey, CA**

Giant Chewy Cereal Cookies
Makes 6 dozen
2 cups butter or margarine
2 cups sugar
2 cups brown sugar
4 eggs, beaten
2 teaspoons vanilla
2 cups oatmeal
2 cups Rice Krispies or any other cereal
4 cups flour
2 teaspoons baking soda
2 teaspoons baking powder
1 ½ cups raisins
1 ½ cups nuts, wheat germ, raisins, coconut or chocolate chips
      or ¾ cup each of two items

Preheat oven to 350 degrees. Melt butter or margarine in large saucepan. Add sugars and stir until dissolved. Add eggs and vanilla. Stir in cereal. Mix flour, baking soda and baking powder together. Add to moist ingredients. Stir in raisins, nuts, etc. Spoon by tablespoons onto cookie sheets. Bake 10 to 12 minutes.
"This recipe came from close friends of my parents. I've yet to try any of their recipes that aren't excellent. Try this, you'll see!"
Connie Sweet   **Rim Of The World High School**
                                                      Lake Arrowhead, CA

Hazelnut Biscotti With Black Pepper

Makes 32

3 cups hazelnuts
2 tablespoons anise seeds, toasted
3 ½ cups flour, unsifted
1 teaspoon baking soda
1 teaspoon baking powder
¼ teaspoon salt
3 teaspoons black pepper
2 sticks unsalted butter, room temperature
2 cups sugar
4 eggs
2 teaspoons lemon zest
2 teaspoons orange zest
1 tablespoon rum
½ small bottle anise extract

Preheat oven to 350 degrees. Place hazelnuts on a baking sheet and roast until lightly browned, about 12 minutes. Roll warm nuts in a dish towel to remove skins; chop coarsely and set aside. Place anise seeds on cookie sheet and roast until lightly browned. Remove from oven and allow to cool; set aside. In a medium bowl, sift together flour, baking soda, baking powder, salt and pepper. In a large bowl, beat butter and sugar with an electric mixer at medium speed, until light and fluffy, about 3 minutes. Add eggs, one at a time, beating well after each addition. Beat in lemon and orange zests, rum, anise extract and anise seeds. Using a rubber spatula, fold in hazelnuts and sifted dry ingredients just until incorporated. Cover and refrigerate overnight. On a lightly floured work surface, shape dough into (2) 12" logs, 1 ½" wide and 1" thick. Place logs on a large heavy buttered baking sheet about 4" apart. Bake in middle of oven for 25 minutes, or until logs are lightly browned and feel firm when pressed in center. Let cool on baking sheet about 10 minutes. Carefully transfer logs to a cutting board. Using a serrated knife, cut them crosswise into ¾" slices. Arrange slices, cut side down, on cookie sheet and bake 15 minutes, until golden brown. Store up to 2 weeks in an airtight container.

Stephanie San Sebastian   **Central High School, Fresno, CA**

Hazelnut Florentines

Makes 25

6 tablespoons butter, cut into pieces
⅓ cup sugar
2 tablespoons light corn syrup
2 tablespoons heavy cream
Scant 1 cup hazelnuts, finely chopped
¼ cup oatmeal
1 cup chocolate chips
1 to 2 teaspoons shortening

Preheat oven to 375 degrees. Line baking sheets with parchment paper. In a medium saucepan, combine butter, sugar, corn syrup and heavy cream. Over medium-high heat, bring mixture to a boil. Stir in hazelnuts and oatmeal. Cook until mixture browns slightly, about 3 minutes. Remove from heat and drop by rounded teaspoonfuls, 3" apart, onto baking sheet. Bake 4 to 6 minutes, one sheet at a time, or until batter spreads and browns lightly around the edges (cookies will appear pale in the center, but change color as they cool). Remove from oven, slide parchment paper off cookie sheet to allow cookies to cool, about 10 minutes. Remove cookies from parchment paper to rack. Melt chocolate chips using enough shortening to make it smooth. Place melted chocolate in a freezer-weight plastic baggie. Snip a tiny corner of the bag and drizzle chocolate over cookies. When chocolate is firm, store florentines in an airtight container.

"This is THE BEST florentine ever!"

Marion S. Anderson   **A.G.Currie Middle School, Tustin, CA**

Heavenly Chocolate Brownies

Makes 2 dozen
> 1 box German chocolate cake mix
> ¾ cup margarine
> ⅓ cup evaporated milk
> 60 caramels
> ½ cup evaporated milk
> 1 cup walnuts, chopped
> 1 cup chocolate chips

Preheat oven to 350 degrees. Mix together first 3 ingredients. Put half of the mixture into a greased 9" x 13" pan and bake 6 minutes. In separate pan, melt together caramels and evaporated milk. Sprinkle chopped walnuts and chocolate chips over baked mixture; pour melted caramel mixture over and then spread remaining cake mixture on top. Bake 15 to 20 minutes.

"These brownies are awesome warm, topped with vanilla ice cream. You cannot eat just one!"

Nicole Rehmann   **La Mesa Junior High School, Santa Clarita, CA**

Hershey's Giant Chocolate Chip Cookie

Serves 8 - 10
> 6 tablespoons (¾ stick) butter or margarine, softened
> ½ cup sugar
> ¼ cup light brown sugar, firmly packed
> ½ teaspoon vanilla
> 1 egg
> 1 cup all-purpose flour
> ½ teaspoon baking soda
> 1 ⅔ cups Hershey's Semi-Sweet Chocolate Chips, MINI CHIPS Semi-Sweet Chocolate, Milk Chocolate Chips, or ALMOND JOY Coconut & Almond Bits

Preheat oven to 350 degrees. Line 12" metal pizza pan with foil. In medium bowl, beat butter, sugar, brown sugar and vanilla until fluffy; add egg, beating well. Stir together flour and baking soda; stir into mixture with chocolate chips. Spread batter evenly in prepared pan, spreading to 1" from edge. Bake 20 to 25 minutes or until lightly brown and set. Cool completely; carefully lift cookie from pan and remove foil. Decorate as desired; cut into wedges to serve.

Perfectly Chocolate Giant Chocolate Chip Cookie: Stir in ⅓ cup Hershey's Cocoa or Hershey's European Style Cocoa with flour mixture.

Hershey Foods Corp.   **Hershey, PA**

Iowa Holiday Cookies

Makes 6 dozen
>1 cup butter or margarine
>1 cup sugar
>½ cup milk
>1 egg, beaten
>1 cup graham cracker crumbs
>1 cup coconut
>½ cup nuts, chopped
>1 can prepared frosting

Melt butter or margarine in electric fry pan at 200 degrees. Increase to 250 degrees and add sugar, milk, egg and graham cracker crumbs. Cook until thick, stirring constantly; cool. Add coconut and nuts. Line bottom of 9" x 13" pan with whole graham crackers. Spread mixture over crackers, use remaining crackers on top. Press down slightly. Frost and let stand 12 to 24 hours in refrigerator. Cut into small squares and enjoy.

Nan Tisdale   **Silverado High School, Las Vegas, NV**

Jello Cookies

Makes 3 dozen
>3 egg whites
>⅛ teaspoon salt
>¾ cup sugar
>3 ½ tablespoons jello, any flavor
>1 teaspoon vinegar
>1 cup chocolate chips

Preheat oven to 250 degrees. In mixing bowl with electric beater, beat egg whites with salt until foamy. Add sugar and jello; beat until stiff. Add vinegar and chocolate chips, Drop tablespoon size drops of batter onto brown paper. Bake 25 minutes. Turn oven off and leave cookie in oven for 20 minutes. Do not remove cookies from paper until completely cooled.

"Use lime or strawberry jello at Christmas time to make red and green cookies."

Lori Wilson   **A.B. Miller High School, Fontana, CA**

Magic Cookie Bars

Makes 1 dozen
>½ cup butter
>1 ½ cups graham cracker crumbs
>1 (14 ounce) can Eagle brand milk (low fat, if desired)
>1 (6 ounce) package semi-sweet chocolate chips
>1 (3 ounce) bag flaked coconut
>1 cup nuts, chopped

Preheat oven to 350 degrees. In a 13" x 9" pan, melt butter in oven. Sprinkle graham cracker crumbs over melted butter. Pour milk evenly over crumbs. Top evenly with remaining ingredients. Press down gently. Bake 25 to 30 minutes. Cool thoroughly before cutting. Store, loosely covered, in the refrigerator.

"These are good served as a dessert with whipped cream, as well as a cookie bar."

Carolyn Helmle   **Thomas Downey High School, Modesto, CA**

Marbled Fudge Bars

Makes 24 bars
1 cup butter
4 (1 ounce) squares unsweetened chocolate
2 cups sugar
3 eggs
1 cup flour
½ teaspoon salt
1 teaspoon vanilla
8 ounces cream cheese, softened
½ cup sugar
1 egg
1 teaspoon vanilla

Preheat oven to 350 degrees. Melt butter and chocolate in heavy saucepan; remove from heat. Add sugar and eggs and beat until combined. Stir in flour, salt and vanilla. Pour into greased 9" x 13" pan. With electric mixer, mix cream cheese, sugar, egg and vanilla in mixing bowl until smooth. With large spoon, drop mixture over all areas of chocolate batter. Using knife, swirl cream cheese mixture through chocolate. Bake 40 to 45 minutes.

Betty Wells   **Bidwell Junior High School, Chico, CA**

Mattie's Ginger Snaps

Makes 3 dozen
¾ cup butter or margarine
1 cup sugar
1 egg
4 tablespoons molasses
2 cups flour
1 teaspoon baking soda
½ teaspoon salt
1 teaspoon cinnamon
½ teaspoon cloves
1 teaspoon ginger

Preheat oven to 350 degrees. Cream butter and sugar. Add egg and molasses. Slowly add dry ingredients. Roll into 1" balls; roll in sugar and press with a fork. Bake 8 minutes for soft cookies; 12 to 15 minutes for harder cookies.

"These ginger snaps are one of my favorite cookies, and I always eat too many. They're so good! I prefer the soft version."

Karen Peters   **Vaca Pena Middle School, Vacaville, CA**

Monster M&M Cookies

Makes 15 giant cookies

2 ¼ cups flour
¾ teaspoon baking powder
½ teaspoon salt
1 cup unsalted butter, softened
¾ cup sugar
½ cup light brown sugar, firmly packed
2 eggs
2 teaspoons vanilla
2 cups M&M's + extra for topping

Preheat oven to 300 degrees. Combine flour, baking powder and salt in large bowl; set aside. Cream butter and sugars together with electric mixer until light and fluffy. Add eggs, beating well after each. Add vanilla; mix well. Spoon flour into butter mixture; beat until smooth. Stir in M&M candies. Drop batter, using ⅓ cup measure, 3 inches apart on ungreased baking sheet. Press additional M&M's into top of each mound. Bake 30 to 35 minutes, allowing to cool 5 minutes before removing from pan to cooling rack.

"A favorite with everyone!"

Sonja Tyree   **Ayala High School, Chino Hills, CA**

Oatmeal Carmelitas

Makes 24

2 cups flour
2 cups quick cooking oatmeal
1 ½ cups brown sugar, firmly packed
1 teaspoon baking soda
½ teaspoon salt
1 cup butter or margarine, melted
1 cup chocolate chips
1 cup nuts, chopped
1 (14 ounce) package wrapped caramels
½ cup light cream

Preheat oven to 350 degrees. In a large mixing bowl, combine flour, oatmeal, brown sugar, baking soda, salt and butter. Mix well and press half of the mixture into greased 9" x 13" pan. Bake 10 minutes; remove from oven. Sprinkle chocolate chips and nuts over oatmeal layer. In a heavy saucepan, melt caramels with cream. Spread caramel mixture over chocolate chips and sprinkle remaining crumb mixture over top. Bake 15 to 20 minutes. Cool, then refrigerate 1 to 2 hours before cutting.

Beth Cropsey-Guerrero   **Selma High School, Selma, CA**

Peanut Butter Chews

Makes 24

⅓ cup butter or margarine
½ cup brown sugar, firmly packed
1 cup sugar
½ cup peanut butter
2 eggs

1 ⅛ teaspoons vanilla
1 cup flour
1 teaspoon baking powder
½ teaspoon salt
½ cup coconut
½ cup powdered sugar, sifted
2 to 3 tablespoons milk

Preheat oven to 350 degrees. Mix together butter, sugar, brown sugar, peanut butter, eggs and vanilla with electric mixer. In separate bowl, combine flour, baking powder, salt and coconut. Add dry ingredients to sugar-butter mixture; mix well. Pour batter into a greased 9" x 13" pan. Bake 25 minutes. Combine powdered sugar and milk; drizzle over hot cookies. Cool and cut into squares.

Laurie Owen　　　　　　　　　　**Challenger Middle School, San Diego, CA**

Peanut Butter Cups

Makes 3 ½ dozen
1 cup butter or margarine
1 cup creamy peanut butter
3 ½ to 4 cups powdered sugar
1 package graham crackers, crushed
2 cups chocolate chips

Cream together butter or margarine and peanut butter. Add powdered sugar and cream well. Add crushed graham crackers to mixture and mix well. Press into a 9" x 13" pan. Melt chocolate chips and spread over top of mixture. Refrigerate until chocolate is firm. Cut or chip into bite-sized pieces.

"Good and rich - tastes like Reese's. These cookies are always the first to go!"

Linda Olsen　　　　　　　　　**Delta High School, Clarksburg, CA**

Peanut Butter Temptations

Makes 48
½ cup butter
½ cup peanut butter
½ cup sugar
½ cup brown sugar
1 egg
1 teaspoon vanilla
1 ¼ cups flour
¾ teaspoon baking soda
½ teaspoon salt
1 package miniature Reese's peanut butter cups (about 40 to a package)

Preheat oven to 375 degrees. Cream butter, peanut butter and sugars. Beat in egg and vanilla; mix well. Sift dry ingredients and blend. Shape dough into 1" balls. Place in ungreased miniature muffin tins. Bake 8 - 10 minutes. Remove and immediately press peanut butter cup into each until only the top shows. Let set awhile before removing from tin.

Pamela Campion　　　　　　　　**Dublin High School, Dublin, CA**

Pecan Tarts

Makes 36
Crust:
6 ounces cream cheese
½ pound butter
2 cups flour
Filling:
3 eggs, beaten well
3 tablespoons butter, melted, cooled
2 cups light brown sugar
1 teaspoon vanilla
Dash salt
Topping:
1 cup pecans, chopped

Preheat oven to 350 degrees. Crust: Mix ingredients together in large mixing bowl with pastry blender until crumbly. Form into large marbles, using floured fingers. Place in muffin tins and press down on bottom and ½ way up sides of muffin tins. Filling: Mix ingredients in a large mixing bowl. Fill the crust lined muffin tins ½ full. Sprinkle with 1 teaspoon chopped pecans. Bake 15 to 20 minutes. Cool before taking out of pans.

NOTE: These can be made a day in advance.
"This recipe was given to me by my Mom, who is one great cook!"
Susan Lefler   **Ramona Junior High School, Chino, CA**

Persimmon Bars

Makes 6 dozen
4 eggs
½ cup vegetable oil
2 cups sugar
2 cups persimmon pulp
2 cups flour
2 teaspoons ground cinnamon
¾ teaspoon ground ginger
¾ teaspoon ground cloves
¾ teaspoon ground nutmeg
¾ teaspoon salt
2 teaspoons baking powder
1 teaspoon baking soda
Frosting:
1 (3 ounce) package cream cheese, softened
2 tablespoons butter or margarine, softened
1 ½ teaspoons milk
½ teaspoon vanilla
¾ teaspoon orange peel, grated
2 cups powdered sugar

Preheat oven to 350 degrees. In large bowl of electric mixer, beat eggs lightly. Beat in oil, sugar and persimmon. In another bowl, stir together flour, cinnamon, ginger, cloves, nutmeg, salt, baking powder and baking soda. Gradually add to persimmon mixture, blending thoroughly. Pour batter into a greased and floured 10" x 15" rimmed baking pan. Bake about 35 minutes, or until edges begin to pull away from pan sides and center springs back when lightly touched. Let cool in pan on a rack. Frosting: In small bowl of electric mixer, beat cream cheese and butter or margarine until fluffy. Beat in milk, vanilla and orange peel. Gradually sift in enough powdered sugar (about 2 cups) to make a spreadable icing. Spread over cooled cookies. Cut into 1" x 2" bars.

Ruth Schletewitz   **Rafer Johnson Junior High School**
                                                              Kingsburg, CA

Pineapple Squares
Makes 18 squares

    1 tablespoon butter
    1 tablespoon sugar
    1 cup flour
    ¼ teaspoon salt
    3 teaspoons baking powder
    3 eggs, well beaten
    1 cup crushed pineapple, well drained
    1 cup sugar
    1 tablespoon butter, melted
    2 cups moist shredded coconut

Preheat oven to 350 degrees. Cream 1 tablespoon butter and 1 tablespoon sugar. Sift together flour, salt and baking powder; add to creamed mixture and mix until crumbly. Beat together eggs; add half of the eggs to creamed mixture and spread into a greased 8" square pan. Spread pineapple over top. Mix 1 cup sugar with melted butter and coconut. Add remaining eggs and mix well; spread over pineapple and bake 30 to 35 minutes. Cool before cutting.

"I like this during Christmas. It can be enjoyed all year."

April Rosendahl   **Chino High School, Chino, CA**

Pudding Cookies For Kids
Makes 2 to 3 dozen

    1 cup Bisquick
    1 small package instant pudding, any flavor
    ¼ cup vegetable oil
    1 egg
    4 ounces: chocolate chips, raisins, nuts, coconut or ⅓ cup peanut butter

Preheat oven to 350 degrees. Mix together Bisquick, pudding mix, oil and egg. Stir in desired addition and roll into balls. Place on ungreased cookie sheet. Dip bottom of a glass in sugar and press it onto each cookie. Decorate with candies before baking, if desired.

"Great recipe for young children or beginning cooks. Easy to do!"

Linda Robinson   **Royal High School, Simi Valley, CA**

Pumpkin Brownies

Serves 10 - 12

Crust:
1 box yellow cake mix (reserve 1 cup)
1 egg, beaten
½ cup butter, melted
Filling:
1 (29 ounce) can pumpkin mix
2 eggs, beaten
⅔ cup (5 ounce) can evaporated milk
Topping:
1 cup (reserved) cake mix
¼ cup sugar
1 tablespoon cinnamon
¼ cup butter
½ cup walnuts, chopped (optional)
Whipped cream (optional)

Preheat oven to 350 degrees. Crust: Combine cake mix (reserving 1 cup), 1 beaten egg, and melted butter in a bowl; blend with a fork to make dough. Press gently into a 13" x 9" x 2", ungreased pan; set aside. Filling: In a large bowl combine pumpkin pie mix, 2 beaten eggs, and milk; blend well and pour over crust. Topping: In a small bowl, combine 1 cup reserved cake mix, sugar, cinnamon, and ¼ cup melted butter; blend until crumbly and sprinkle on top of filling. Top with chopped walnuts, if desired. Bake 1 hour and 20 minutes or until toothpick inserted in center comes out clean. Cool slightly. Cut into squares. Serve warm with or without whipped cream.

*"This is one of those favorite recipes passed around the office while
my mother was working. Thanks Mom for sharing it with me."*

Gerry Henderson   **Temple City High School, Temple City, CA**

Raisin Ribbon Bars

Serves 16

½ cup butter or margarine, softened
⅔ cup brown sugar, firmly packed
½ cup flour
1 ½ cups oats
1 cup walnuts, chopped
1 cup raisins
½ cup jam or preserves, any flavor

Preheat oven to 375 degrees. Beat together butter and brown sugar. Stir in flour, oats and walnuts. Reserve 1 cup batter for topping. Press remaining batter into lightly greased 8" square pan. Combine raisins and jam. Spread to within ½" of edges. Sprinkle with reserved batter; press lightly. Bake 25 to 30 minutes.

*"I found this easy and delicious recipe and made it three different
times with different jams, but strawberry is the best."*

Gail Hurt Kniereiem   **Estancia High School, Costa Mesa, CA**

Raspberry Crumbles

Makes 24 squares

2 ¼ cups flour
1 ½ cups sugar
¾ cup pecans, chopped
1 cup butter, softened
1 egg
1 cup seedless raspberry jam

Preheat oven to 350 degrees. Using an electric mixer, mix flour, sugar, pecans, butter and egg for 3 minutes. (Mixture will be crumbly.) Reserve 1 ½ cups mixture; set aside. Press mixture into an 8" x 8" square, greased pan. Spread jam on top and sprinkle reserved mixture over top. Bake 40 to 50 minutes.

Shelly Wellins   **Bolsa Grande High School, Garden Grove, CA**

Rocky Road Fudge Bars

Makes 24

Brownie:
1 square unsweetened chocolate
½ cup margarine or butter
1 cup sugar
1 cup flour
½ cup nuts, chopped
1 teaspoon baking powder
1 teaspoon vanilla
2 eggs
Filling:
6 ounces cream cheese, softened
½ cup sugar
2 tablespoons flour
¼ cup butter or margarine
1 egg
½ teaspoon vanilla
¼ cup nuts, chopped
Frosting:
2 cups miniature marshmallows
¼ cup butter or margarine
1 ounce unsweetened chocolate
2 ounces cream cheese
¼ cup milk
3 cups powdered sugar
1 teaspoon vanilla

Preheat oven to 350 degrees. In a large soucepan, melt chocolate and butter over low heat. Remove heat and remaining brownie ingredients; mix well. Spread evenly in bottom of a greased and floured 13" x 9" pan. In mixing bowl, combine filling ingredients and spread over chocolate brownie batter. Bake 25 to 30 minutes or until a toothpick inserted in center comes out clean. Remove from oven and sprinkle with marshmallows; return to oven for 2 minutes more. In a saucepan, heat butter, chocolate, cream cheese and milk over low heat until chocolate melts. Remove from heat and stir in powdered sugar and vanilla. Pour frosting over marshmallows and and swirl. Cool and cut into 24 bars.

"My daughter got this recipe from her friend, Melissa. It's a tradition to make them together. They're good without the nuts too!"

Larkin Evans   **Half Moon Bay High School, Half Moon Bay, CA**

Salted Peanut Chews

Makes 36

Crust:
1 ½ cups flour
⅔ cup brown sugar, firmly packed
½ teaspoon baking powder
½ teaspoon salt
¼ teaspoon baking soda
½ cup butter or margarine, softened
1 teaspoon vanilla
2 egg yolks
3 cups salted peanuts
½ package miniature marshmallows
Topping:
⅔ cup corn syrup
¼ cup butter or margarine
2 teaspoons vanilla
1 (10 ounce) package peanut butter chips
2 cups crisp rice cereal
2 cups salted peanuts

Preheat oven to 350 degrees. Lightly spoon flour into measure cup, level off. In large bowl, combine all crust ingredients, except marshmallows, at low speed until crumbly. Press firmly into bottom of ungreased 13" x 9" pan. Bake 12 to 15 minutes, or until lightly golden brown. Remove from oven and immediately sprinkle with marshmallows. Return to oven; bake an additional 1 to 2 minutes or until marshmallows just begin to puff. Cool while preparing topping. In large saucepan, combine all topping ingredients, except cereal and peanuts. Heat just until chips are melted and mixture is smooth, stirring constantly. Remove from heat; stir in cereal and peanuts. Immediately spoon warm topping over marshmallows; spread to cover. Refrigerate 45 minutes or until firm. Cut into bars.

"This recipe was a hit at the Christmas Tea given by the students."

Darlene Lupul   **Tokay High School, Lodi, CA**

Scottish Shortbread

Makes 3 - 4 dozen
1 pound butter (4 cubes)
1 cup sugar
5 cups flour

Preheat oven to 300 degrees. Roll sugar with rolling pin to make sugar fine. Mix butter and sugar together. Add flour 1 cup at a time. Work with hands and knead dough thoroughly many times. Roll ⅓ of dough out on to floured board and cut into oblong squares about 1" x 4". Prick with fork. Lay on brown paper on cookie sheet and bake 30 minutes, checking to make sure they don't brown. Repeat with remaining dough.

"We make this even better by dipping ½ cookie in chocolate. Yum!"

Debbie Thompson   **Foothill High School, Tustin, CA**

Sensible Chocolate Chip Cookies

Makes 5 dozen

1 ¼ cups brown sugar, firmly packed
½ cup sugar
½ cup I Can't Believe It's Not Butter margarine
1 teaspoon vanilla
2 egg whites
3 cups all-purpose flour
1 ½ teaspoons baking soda
1 teaspoon salt
⅓ cup water
2 cups lowfat chocolate chips
Nonfat cooking spray

Preheat oven to 350 degrees. Cream sugars, margarine and vanilla in mixing bowl, beat in egg whites. In separate bowl, combine flour, baking soda and salt. Add dry ingredients, alternately with water, to creamed mixture. Stir in chocolate chips. Spray cookie sheet with nonstick cooking spray and drop batter by rounded tablespoonfuls. Bake 10 to 12 minutes.

NOTE: Dough refrigerates well.

"Students made about 20 dozen for Founder's Day Celebration. They were enjoyed by everyone."

Janet Riegel   **Charter Oak High School, Covina, CA**

Snickerdoodles

Makes 4 - 5 dozen

1 ¼ cups + 2 tablespoons flour
1 teaspoon cream of tartar
½ teaspoon soda
½ teaspoon salt
½ cup shortening
¾ cup sugar
1 egg
Topping:
1 teaspoon cinnamon
2 tablespoons sugar

Preheat oven to 350 degrees. Measure flour, cream of tartar, soda and salt in sifter; sift and set aside. Mix together shortening, sugar and egg. Use electric mixer until mixture is creamy. Slowly mix dry ingredients with wet. Add a small amount at a time until all dry ingredients are thoroughly blended. Mix cinnamon and sugar together in bowl. Roll dough into balls the size of walnuts. Roll in cinnamon-sugar. Place 2 inches apart on ungreased cookie sheet and bake 8 to 10 minutes.

"Everyone loves snickerdoodles, especially my students!"

Penny Childers   **Ramona High School, Ramona, CA**

87

Spanish Peanut Cookies

Makes 5 dozen

1 ½ cups flour
¼ teaspoon baking powder
½ teaspoon baking soda
1 cup brown sugar
1 cup shortening
1 egg, beaten
½ teaspoon vanilla
½ cup cornflake crumbs
1 ¼ cups oatmeal
1 cup Spanish peanuts

Preheat oven to 350 degrees. Sift flour, measure, then add baking powder and baking soda; sift twice and set aside. In mixing bowl, add brown sugar slowly to shortening; beat in egg and vanilla. Add sifted flour mixture. Stir in cornflake crumbs, oatmeal and peanuts; mix well. Drop onto ungreased cookie sheets and bake 15 minutes.

"I got this recipe from my 7th grade Home Economics teacher. It has been a family favorite ever since. With all of the "healthy ingredients", it makes a good "lunch box" treat!"

Carolyn McBride   **Arcadia High School, Arcadia, CA**

The Best Chocolate Chip Cookies

Makes 2 dozen

⅓ cup shortening
⅓ cup butter
½ cup sugar
½ cup brown sugar
1 egg
1 teaspoon vanilla
1 ½ cups flour
½ teaspoon baking soda
½ teaspoon salt
½ cup nuts (optional)
1 cup chocolate chips

Preheat oven to 375 degrees. Mix the first six ingredients together thoroughly. Gradually add remaining ingredients and mix well. Drop by large spoonfuls on to cookie sheet. (I use a cookie scoop). Bake 8 to 10 minutes.

"Everyone that has eaten these cookies loves them! My daughters, Courtney and Summer, love to make these and eat them."

Jeri Drake Lane   **Canyon Springs High School**
                                                       Moreno Valley, CA

The Best Ever Ranger Cookies

Makes 2 to 3 dozen

½ cup margarine
½ cup sugar
½ cup brown sugar
½ teaspoon vanilla
1 egg
1 cup all-purpose flour
½ teaspoon soda
¼ teaspoon baking powder
¼ teaspoon salt
1 cup quick cooking oats
1 cup honey oats or almond flaked cereal
½ cup coconut, shredded
½ cup raisins

Preheat oven to 350 degrees. Cream margarine and sugars until fluffy. Add vanilla and eggs, beating until well blended. Stir in remaining ingredients. Drop dough by rounded teaspoonfuls 2" apart onto ungreased cookie sheet. Bake 10 minutes. Immediately remove from baking sheet. When cool, store in sealed container.

"Whenever I ask what kind of cookies to make, everyone requests these. They won't last long so make a double recipe."

Maria Hoffman   **Katella High School, Anaheim, CA**

Triple Chocolate Cookies

Makes 22

⅔ cup butter, softened
⅔ cup sugar
⅓ cup brown sugar, firmly packed
1 egg
1 teaspoon vanilla
2 ounces unsweetened chocolate, melted
1 ½ cups flour
1 ½ cups Swiss dark chocolate, chopped
1 (5 ounce) bar white chocolate, chopped

Preheat oven to 325 degrees. Lightly grease cookie sheet. In large bowl, beat butter, sugars, egg, vanilla and melted chocolate at medium-high speed until fluffy. Gradually add flour. Stir in dark and white chocolate. Drop heaping teaspoonfuls of dough onto cookie sheet. Bake 17 minutes or until top looks dry.

"Delicious!"

Brenda Umbro   **Orange Glen High School, Escondido, CA**

Walnut Macaroons

Makes 2 ½ dozen
¼ cup flour
⅔ cup sugar
¼ teaspoon salt
2 ⅔ cups flaked coconut
4 large egg whites
1 teaspoon black walnut extract
1 cup walnuts, chopped

Preheat oven to 325 degrees. Combine flour, sugar, salt and coconut. Stir in egg whites and walnut extract. Stir in walnuts; mix well. Drop by teaspoonfuls onto greased cookie sheet. Bake 20 to 25 minutes or until golden brown. Remove to cooling racks.

"Light, chewy, great for holiday."

Nancy Albers **Lassen High School, Susanville, CA**

Frozen Treats

Baked Alaska

Serves 6

1 loaf pound cake
1 gallon ice cream, any flavor
3 egg whites
½ teaspoon vanilla
¼ teaspoon cream of tartar
6 tablespoons sugar

Slice pound cake. Slice ice cream and place on cake slices alternately on ovenproof plate. Beat egg whites with vanilla and cream of tartar until soft peaks form. Gradually add sugar, beating until stiff and glossy peaks form and all sugar is dissolved. Frost ice cream-cake slices completely with meringue and freeze. When ready to serve, heat oven to 500 degrees. Bake 3 to 5 minutes, until meringue is golden brown.

"Easy to make and a great way to awe your guests."

Barbara Crampton   **Buena Park High School, Buena Park, CA**

Baked Alaska

Serves 12 - 16

9" round layer sponge cake, any flavor
Half gallon ice cream, any flavor
6 large egg whites
½ teaspoon cream of tartar
1 cup sugar

Use a round bowl that's about 1" smaller than layer cake; line it with plastic wrap. Pack ice cream into bowl and place in freezer several hours before serving. Place cake in refrigerator several hours, until well chilled. Preheat oven to 450 degrees. Place a cutting board on a cookie sheet. Shortly before serving, beat egg whites with cream of tartar until frothy. Gradually beat in sugar. Continue beating until meringue is stiff and glossy. Place cooled layer of cake on cutting board, invert bowl with ice cream onto cake; remove bowl and plastic wrap. Cover cake and ice cream with meringue, sealing meringue to board for a complete seal. Bake 3 to 5 minutes, until meringue is delicately browned. Serve immediately.

"Make sure your oven is preheated at least 20 minutes before baking. Your ice cream needs to be frozen solid and cake should be cold. Don't peak meringue because peaks will burn. Work fast."

Jane Greaves   **Central High School, Fresno, CA**

Chocolate Wafer Log

Serves 12

2 cups (1 pint) heavy whipping cream OR 8 ounces Cool Whip
1 tablespoon sugar
1 (9 ounce) package Nabisco Famous Chocolate Wafers
Garnish: chocolate and/or colored sprinkles

Whip the whipping cream and sugar, if using, or use Cool Whip. Spread a spoonful of whipped cream on each wafer. Stack wafers on edge, in a row, on a serving platter to make a 14" log. Frost with remaining whipped cream. Chill 4 to 6 hours or overnight. To serve, garnish with chocolate or colored sprinkles. Slice log at a 45 degree angle.

> *"This is really Nabisco's recipe, but it has been our family favorite for years."*

Julie Hampton   **Gresham High School, Gresham, OR**

Coffee Can Ice Cream

Serves 4-5

1 cup whole milk
1 cup whipping cream
½ cup sugar
1 teaspoon vanilla extract
1 egg, beaten (optional)
Nuts or fruits, as desired
Crushed ice
Rock salt

Put all ingredients into a 1 pound coffee can with a tight-fitting lid. Place lid on can. Place can with ingredients inside a 2 ½ pound coffee can with tight fitting lid. Pack large can with crushed ice around smaller can. Pour at least ¾ cup rock salt evenly over ice. Place lid on large can. Roll can back and forth on CEMENT SLAB for ten minutes. Open outer can; remove inner can; remove lid. Us a rubber spatula to stir and scrape sides of can. Replace lid. Drain water from large can; insert small can and repack with ice and salt. Roll 5 minutes more.

> *"This is a recipe I learned during my years as a Girl Scout leader, and now my students love making ice cream during hot weather. The egg makes a richer ice cream, but we omit it because of the salmonella danger."*

Ellen Gordon   **Colton High School, Colton, CA**

Frozen Lemon Cream with Raspberry Purée

Serves 10 - 12

Crust:
1 package graham cracker crumbs
6 tablespoons butter, melted
Lemon Cream:
3 cups whipping cream
½ cup fresh lemon juice
1 ¼ cups sugar
3 tablespoons lemon peel, grated
Topping:
6 ounces raspberries, frozen
¾ cup water

½ cup sugar
Garnish: whipped cream, optional

Preheat oven to 350 degrees. Crust: Combine graham cracker crumbs and melted butter. Pat onto bottom and 1" up sides of 10" springform pan. Bake 10 minutes; cool. Lemon cream: Mix whipping cream, lemon juice, sugar and lemon peel until blended and slightly thickened. Pour over baked crust and cover with foil. Freeze overnight or up to one month. Do not thaw before serving. To serve, remove sides of springform pan. Topping: Purée raspberries together with sugar and water. Spread topping over center of pie or cut individual slices and spoon sauce over each slice. Garnish with whipped cream, if desired.

"You'll have many requests for this recipe."

Carol Goddard   **Alhambra High School, Alhambra, CA**

Frozen Pumpkin Pecan Pie
Serves 6 - 8

1 quart butter pecan ice cream
1 cup canned pumpkin pie filling
¼ cup sugar
¼ teaspoon cinnamon
⅛ teaspoon ginger
Dash nutmeg
1 baked graham cracker crust pie shell

Soften ice cream just until easily stirred. Combine ice cream with pie filling, sugar, cinnamon, ginger and nutmeg, stirring until well blended. Spoon into cooled crust. Cover with plastic wrap and freeze for several hours until firm.

"Guests like this pie and often ask for my recipe."

Wanda Shelton   **Newport Harbor High School, Newport Beach, CA**

Holiday Ice Cream Squares
Serves 10 - 12

2 cups canned pumpkin
1 cup sugar
1 teaspoon salt
1 teaspoon cinnamon
1 teaspoon nutmeg
1 cup walnuts, chopped
½ gallon vanilla ice cream, softened
36 gingersnaps, crushed
Whipped cream, for topping

Combine pumpkin, sugar, salt, cinnamon and nutmeg; mix well and stir in walnuts. Place softened ice cream into a chilled bowl. Gently fold pumpkin mixture into ice cream. Line bottom of 13" x 9" x 2" pan with half of the crushed gingersnaps. Cover with half of the ice cream-pumpkin mixture. Repeat layers. Freeze overnight. Cut into squares when ready to serve. Top with whipped cream.

"This is a wonderful change of pace for a Thanksgiving dessert."

Linda Paskins   **Cordova High School, Rancho Cordova, CA**

Ice Cream Dream Dessert

Serves 12

Crust:
1 ½ cups graham cracker crumbs
¼ cup sugar
½ cup butter, melted
Filling:
6 to 8 chocolate bars with almonds
½ cup butter
3 egg yolks, beaten
½ cup powdered sugar
½ cup whole almonds
3 egg whites, stiffly beaten
½ gallon vanilla or fudge-ripple ice cream

Preheat oven to 375 degrees. Mix together crust ingredients and press 1 ¼ cups of mixture into bottom of a 9" x 13" pan. Reserve remainder of mixture for crumb topping. Bake 6 minutes; remove from oven and cool. Filling: Melt chocolate bars and butter slowly in saucepan or over double boiler. Combine chocolate mixture with egg yolks and cook over low heat 3 minutes. Add powdered sugar and nuts. Cool mixture. Beat egg whites until stiff. Add egg whites to cooled mixture. Spread softened ice cream on cooled crumb crust. Spread chocolate mixture over ice cream. Sprinkle reserved graham cracker crumb mixture on top of chocolate. Freeze until ready to use. Soften slightly before cutting into squares.

Wendy Johnson   **Temecula Valley High School, Temecula, CA**

Ice Cream Pumpkin Pie

Serves 6 - 8

1 pint vanilla ice cream
1 (9") pastry shell, baked
1 (16 ounce) can pumpkin
1 ½ cups sugar
1 teaspoon ground ginger
1 teaspoon ground cinnamon
1 teaspoon vanilla extract
1 ½ cups whipping cream, divided
Caramelized Almonds:
¼ cup sugar
1 cup almonds, slivered

Spread ice cream in bottom of pastry shell; freeze. Combine pumpkin, sugar, ginger, cinnamon and vanilla. In separate bowl, beat 1 cup whipping cream until soft peaks form. Mix with pumpkin mixture and pour over ice cream layer. Cover and freeze. Meanwhile, combine sugar and almonds in a large skillet; cook over low heat, stirring constantly, until sugar melts and almonds are lightly browned. Spread almond mixture in a thin layer on a buttered baking sheet; cool, then break into small pieces. Beat remaining ½ cup whipping cream until soft peaks form. Spoon around edge of pie. Sprinkle with caramelized almonds. Serve immediately.

Ruth Nixon   **Scripps Ranch High School, San Diego, CA**

Ice Cream Supra

Serves 12

4 ounces almonds, slivered
½ cup butter
1 cup brown sugar
1 cup coconut, shredded
2 ½ cups Rice Chex cereal, crushed
½ gallon vanilla ice cream, softened (rectangular box shape is best)

Saute almonds in butter. In a bowl, mix together brown sugar, coconut and crushed cereal. Add sauteed almonds and mix thoroughly. Spread half of the mixture into a 9" x 13" pan. Smooth ice cream over mixture. Top with remaining mixture. Put in freezer to chill.

Pat Smith **Kern Valley High School, Lake Isabella, CA**

Mocha Punch

Makes 5 quarts

1 ½ quarts water
½ cup instant chocolate drink mix
½ cup sugar
¼ cup instant coffee granules
½ gallon vanilla ice cream
½ gallon chocolate ice cream
Garnish: whipped cream, chocolate curls

In large saucepan, bring water to a boil. Remove from heat. Add drink mix, sugar and coffee; stir until dissolved. Cover and refrigerate 4 hours or overnight. About 30 minutes before serving, pour into a punch bowl. Add ice cream by scoopfuls; stir until partially melted. Garnish with dollops of whipped cream and chocolate curls, if desired.

"Tastes like a chocolate malt punch with a light mocha flavor. My class voted this a 'keeper' ".

Carol Goddard **Alhambra High School, Alhambra, CA**

Oreo Ice Cream

Serves 6 - 8

2 ¼ cups sugar
4 eggs
½ teaspoon salt
5 cups milk
4 ½ teaspoons vanilla
4 cups half & half
24 Oreo cookies, broken into fourths

In large bowl, beat together sugar, eggs and salt. Heat milk; do not boil. Add milk slowly to egg mixture. Return to heat and cook on low, stirring constantly for 5 minutes. Remove from heat; cool 15 minutes. Add vanilla, half & half and Oreos. Freeze in ice cream maker according to manufacturers instructions.

"My sister, Margie, gave me this recipe years ago. It is a summer favorite with friends and family. The ice cream turns out chocolatey with chunks of cookies in it."

Cheryl McDaniels **Green Valley High School, Henderson, NV**

Party Lemonade

Makes 2 quarts

1 cup sugar
1 ¼ cups water
1 ¼ cups fresh lemon juice (about 8 large lemons)
1 cup fresh raspberries
1 pint pineapple sherbet
3 cups carbonated water, chilled

Bring sugar and 1 ¼ cups water to a boil in small saucepan. Boil, stirring occasionally, 2 minutes or until sugar dissolves; cool completely. Combine cooled syrup, lemon juice and raspberries; cover and chill at least 2 hours. Scoop sherbet into punch bowl or pitcher just before serving. Combine juice mixture and carbonated water; pour over sherbet.

"Great for a spring baby or wedding shower."

Julie Shelburne   **Tulare Union High School, Tulare, CA**

Rainbow Delight

Serves 12 - 16

18 coconut macaroons
1 ½ pints heavy whipping cream
1 cup pecans, chopped, divided
1 pint orange sherbet, softened
1 pint lime sherbet, softened
1 pint raspberry sherbet, softened
1 ½ cups toasted coconut

Crumble macaroons. Whip cream until stiff. Fold in macaroons and ½ cup pecans. Pour ½ mixture into foil lined 13" x 9" pan. Spoon sherbets on top of the cream. Spread remaining half of cream mixture over sherbet. Sprinkle with coconut and ½ cup pecans. Cover with foil and freeze. Thaw 20 minutes before serving. Keeps up to 4 weeks if using heavy duty foil.

"Pege Graham, Valley High School's favorite volunteer, demonstrated this in her Home Economics class in the 60's. She's still getting A's on it!"

Mary M. Rector   **Valley High School, Las Vegas, NV**

Sharon's Macaroon Dessert

Serves 12 - 16

18 coconut macaroons
1 pint whipping cream
3 tablespoons sugar
1 teaspoon vanilla
½ cup nuts, finely chopped
3 pints sherbet, any flavors, softened

Crumble macaroons and set aside. Whip whipping cream. Stir in sugar, vanilla, macaroons and nuts. Mix together and spread ½ of mixture into an 11" x 17" pan. Spread with sherbets, layering one flavor at a time. Top with remaining macaroon mixture. Freeze overnight. Place in refrigerator one hour before serving.

"Perfect - light & refreshing dessert."

Linda Hsieh   **Rowland High School, Rowland Heights, CA**

Root Beer Cake
Page 36

Crunchy Brunch Cake
Page 22

Try a Smoothie for a Low-Fat Dessert.

Tropical Blueberry Smoothie
page 147

Tin Roof Ice Cream Dessert

Serves 12

1 small package Oreo cookies
½ gallon ice cream (rectangular box shape is best)
1 jar hot fudge sauce
1 can Spanish peanuts
1 small carton Cool Whip

Crush Oreo cookies. Place most in bottom of a large rectangular pan, saving a few for the top. Open all sides of ice cream and slice (ice cream should be frozen solid) into several slices, placing on top of Oreos and pressing into pan. Pour hot fudge sauce on top of ice cream; sprinkle with peanuts. Freeze for 20 minutes, then top with Cool Whip. Sprinkle with remaining crushed Oreos. Freeze at least 1 hour before serving.

"This is so quick and easy, and everyone also asks for the recipe!
It's very rich, so serve small pieces."

Debbie Powers   **Griffiths Middle School, Downey, CA**

Tortoni

Serves 6 - 8

1 ½ cups miniature marshmallows
¼ cup milk
½ cup heavy cream, whipped
¼ cup toasted almonds, chopped
¼ cup maraschino cherries, chopped
½ teaspoon vanilla extract
¼ teaspoon almond extract
1 tablespoon cocoa
¾ teaspoon rum extract

Place marshmallows and milk in large microwave-safe container. Microwave for 45 seconds to 1 minute. Stir until smooth. Chill until slightly thickened. Mix until smooth. Beat heavy cream until soft peaks form. Carefully fold in marshmallow mixture. Divide this mixture in half. To half of the mixture, add toasted almonds, cherries, vanilla and almond extracts. To other half, add cocoa and rum extract. Layer into cupcake paper liners or family dessert dishes. Freeze.

"A nice dessert after an Italian meal."

Susie Pendleton   **Cerritos High School, Cerritos, CA**

Fruits, Cobblers and Gelatins

*A*mbrosia

Serves 10 - 12

    1 cup cream cheese, softened
    1 cup crushed pineapple, drained
    1 cup mandarin orange segments, drained
    1 cup coconut
    1 cup miniature marshmallows

Mix cream cheese with crushed pineapple, Mandarin oranges (reserve a few for garnish), coconut and marshmallows. Spread in glass square pan, garnish with oranges and refrigerate overnight.

"This is a family recipe (over 60 years) enjoyed at every family gathering.
It is attractive in a glass 9" pan and a big hit at pot lucks."

Georgette Phillips   **Silverado High School, Victorville, CA**

*A*pple *C*risp

Serves 6

    5 Granny Smith apples, peeled, cored, thinly sliced
    1 ½ tablespoons fresh lemon juice
    ½ cup flour
    ½ cup oatmeal
    1 cup sugar
    ½ cup pecans, chopped, toasted
    1 ½ teaspoons cinnamon
    ½ teaspoon salt
    ½ cup unsalted butter, cold, cut into pieces

Preheat oven to 350 degrees. Grease an 8" square pan. Mix together apples and lemon juice; place in pan. In food processor, process flour, oatmeal, sugar, cinnamon and salt. Add butter and process, using repeated pulses, until mixture resembles coarse meal. Add pecans and pulse on-off to mix. Press crumb mixture evenly over apples, making sure edges are well sealed. Bake until top is golden and apples are tender, about 1 hour. Serve warm with ice cream.

NOTE: To toast pecans, place in ungreased frying pan and cook until they start to turn a darker color; remove from pan immediately.

Julie Blanchard   **Western High School, Anaheim, CA**

Apple Walnut Cobbler

Serves 8

½ cup sugar
½ teaspoon cinnamon
¾ cup walnuts, chopped
4 cups apples, peeled and sliced
1 cup flour, sifted
1 cup sugar
1 teaspoon baking powder
¼ teaspoon salt
1 egg, well beaten
½ cup evaporated milk
⅓ cup butter, melted
Garnish: whipped cream

Preheat oven to 325 degrees. Mix sugar, cinnamon and ½ cup walnuts; set aside. Put apples in bottom of a greased 8" x 8" or 9" round pan; sprinkle with cinnamon mixture. Sift together dry ingredients. Combine egg, milk and butter. Add dry ingredients all at once and mix until smooth. Pour over apples. Sprinkle with remaining ¼ cup walnuts. Bake until golden brown, about 50 minutes. Serve with whipped cream.

"My mother and I created this recipe when I was in high school,
and I have loved it as a fall treat ever since."

Rebecca Harshbarger   **Temecula Valley High School, Temecula, CA**

Apricot Mousse

Serves 6

1 ½ cups dried apricots
1 cup water
½ cup sugar
1 thin strip yellow lemon rind
1 cup cream, whipped

In small saucepan, combine apricots, water, sugar and lemon rind. Bring to a boil, cover and simmer 20 minutes; cool. Blend apricots and juice in an electric blender for 20 seconds, stopping to stir down if necessary. Fold apricot purée into whipped cream. Spoon into sherbet glasses and chill.

"Peaches are very good in this recipe also!"

Helen Lievre   **La Canada High School, La Canada, CA**

Berry Crisp

Serves 12

6 cups berries
½ to ¾ cup white sugar
¼ cup tapioca granules
1 cup brown sugar
1 cup oats
½ cup flour
¼ cup graham cracker crumbs
1 teaspoon baking soda
1 teaspoon vanilla
½ cup butter or margarine, melted
Vanilla Ice Cream (optional)

Preheat oven to 350 degrees. Mix 2 cups berries with sugar and bring to a boil. Add tapioca granules to thicken and boil until thickened (adding a little water if necessary). Mix the boiled berry mixture with the remaining berries. Pour into baking dish that has been sprayed with nonstick cooking spray. Mix together brown sugar, oats, flour, graham cracker crumbs and baking soda together. Add vanilla and melted butter or margarine and mix until crumbly. Sprinkle over fruit mixture. Bake, uncovered approximately, 30 minutes or until bubbly and topping is golden brown. Serve warm with vanilla ice cream.

"I got this recipe from the Galena Lodge in Ketchum, Idaho."

Teri Ensch   **Serrano High School, Lake Forest, CA**

Chocolate Raspberry Streusel Squares

Makes 36

2 ¼ cups flour
2 ¼ cups oatmeal
¾ cup sugar
¾ cup brown sugar
1 ½ teaspoons baking powder
¾ teaspoon salt
1 ½ cups margarine
1 ½ cups raspberry pre-serves 1 ½ cups chocolate chips
1 cup almonds or walnuts

Preheat oven to 375 degrees. Grease a 9" x 13" pan. In a bowl, combine flour, oats, sugar, brown sugar, baking powder and salt. Cut in margarine until crumbly. Reserve 2 cups mixture for topping later. Press remainder of mixture into bottom of pan. Spread preserves on crust; top with chocolate chips. Add nuts to reserved 2 cups mixture. Sprinkle on top and bake 30 to 35 minutes or until golden brown. Cool; cut into squares.

Debbie Harvey   **Amador Valley High School, Pleasanton, CA**

Country Style Apricot Cobbler

Serves 12

1 ½ quarts ripe apricots, washed, halved, seeded
½ to 1 cup sugar
1 recipe pie crust

Preheat oven to 350 degrees. Place apricot halves in single layer in a 9" x 13" glass baking dish, squeezing them in to fit. According to your taste, pour the amount of sugar desired evenly over apricots. Bake until juice from apricots is boiling and has a syrup-like consistency, about 15 to 20 minutes. Meanwhile, prepare pie crust. Roll out to a rectangle a little larger than the baking dish, about 1/8" thick. Cut out designs if you wish. Remove baking dish from oven. Carefully lift and drape pie crust over boiling apricots, allowing crust to have some graceful folds or bumps. Place back in oven and bake another 15 to 20 minutes, until crust is golden brown.

"*My mother, raised on a farm in Oklahoma, can make the most delicious and gorgeous cobblers in this simple way. Serve with vanilla ice cream for an added treat!*"

Beth Swift   **La Habra High School, La Habra, CA**

Fresh Fruit Taco

Serves 4

3 tablespoons sugar
1 teaspoon ground cinnamon
4 (6") tortillas
2 tablespoons water
Nonstick cooking spray
1 (.3 ounce) package instant sugar free vanilla or chocolate pudding mix
1 teaspoon lemon peel, grated
1 teaspoon vanilla
1 DOLE Banana, peeled, sliced
1 DOLE Mango, peeled, sliced
1 DOLE Kiwi fruit, peeled, sliced
½ cup DOLE Raspberries

Combine sugar and cinnamon. Brush tortillas lightly with water. Sprinkle sugar mixture over both sides of tortillas. Spray large custard cups with nonstick cooking spray. Gently press tortillas into cups. Bake at 400 degrees, 10 minutes or until lightly browned; cool. Prepare pudding according to package directions. Stir lemon peel and vanilla into pudding. Combine banana, mango, kiwi and raspberries in small bowl. Arrange tortilla shells on dessert plates. Spoon about ½ cup pudding into each shell. Spoon fruit onto pudding in shells.

Dole Foods   **San Francisco, CA**

Ice Cream Jello

Serves 6
1 (6 ounce) box jello, any flavor
1 cup boiling water
3 cups vanilla ice cream or ice milk
Garnish: Whipped topping

Combine boiling water and jello in 2 quart bowl. Stir until jello is dissolved. Premeasure 3 cups of ice cream or ice milk; combine with jello and stir until ice cream is completely incorporated into mixture (no lumps of ice cream can be seen). Chill until firm. Top with nondairy whipped topping after jello is set.

"I sprinkle chopped nuts over the topping or place cherries on top to make it look special. Many times I serve this on holidays as a side dish."

Claudia Whitendale   **Strathmore Union High School**

Strathmore, CA

Lime Delight

Serves 10 - 12
1 (13 ounce) can evaporated milk (not lowfat)
1 (3 ounce) package lime jello
1 ¾ cup hot water
¾ cup sugar
¼ cup lime juice
2 teaspoons lemon juice
Green food coloring
2 cups (1 package) Famous Chocolate Wafer crumbs
½ cup margarine, melted
Chocolate chips, for topping

Chill milk in freezer until icy. Dissolve jello in hot water and chill until partially set. Whip jello until fluffy, stir in sugar and fruit juices. Whip milk and fold in jello mixture. Add green food coloring. Mix margarine and cookie crumbs; press into bottom of 9" x 13" pan. Pour jello and milk mixture over top. Decorate with chocolate chips. Chill until firm.

"A light and tasty dessert! The chocolate and lime flavors are a unique and popular combination - a family classic in the Griffenhagen family!"

Gaylen Roe   **Magnolia Junior High School, Chino, CA**

Microwave Apple Crisp

Serves 6 - 8

6 cups apples, cored, peeled and sliced
1 tablespoon lemon juice
1 cup flour
1 cup quick cooking oats
½ cup brown sugar
I teaspoon cinnamon
½ cup butter or margarine, softened

Using a microwave safe baking dish, place prepared apples in an even layer. Sprinkle with lemon juice. Combine flour, oats, brown sugar and cinnamon together in a mixing bowl. Cut in butter or margarine until mixture is crumbly. Sprinkle evenly over apples. Cook on HIGH 12 to 14 minutes or until apples are tender.

"I use this as a lab recipe when the students are studying the Fruit Group.
I usually cut the amounts in half, so it cuts the cooking time in half also."

Roberta Marshall   **Solano Junior High School, Vallejo, CA**

Old Fashioned Apple Crunch

Serves 6 - 8

1 cup brown sugar
1 teaspoon cinnamon
8 tart apples
1 cup sugar
1 cup flour
½ teaspoon salt
1 teaspoon baking powder
1 egg, beaten
½ cup butter or margarine, melted

Preheat oven to 350 degrees. Combine brown sugar and cinnamon; set aside. Peel and slice apples, Place in a greased 9" x 13" baking pan. Sprinkle with ½ of the brown sugar mixture. Combine sugar, flour, salt and baking powder until it resembles crumbs. Stir in beaten egg until mixture looks "crumbly". Spread over apples and sprinkle with remaining brown sugar mixture. Pour butter over top and bake 40 minutes, or until golden brown.

"Serve with ice cream! Yum! This is so good it disappears in seconds. My family and neighbors love it."

Armida Gordon   **Fountain Valley High School, Fountain Valley, CA**

Peach Cobbler

Serves 6

Filling:
½ cup brown sugar
4 teaspoons cornstarch
¼ teaspoon nutmeg
½ cup water
4 cups (about 8 medium) fresh peaches, peeled, sliced
1 tablespoon lemon juice
1 tablespoon margarine
Biscuit Topping:
1 cup flour
2 tablespoons sugar
1 ½ teaspoons baking powder
¼ teaspoon salt
¼ cup margarine
1 egg, slightly beaten
¼ cup milk

Preheat oven to 400 degrees. Filling: Combine brown sugar, cornstarch and nutmeg; stir in water. Cook and stir until thickened and bubbly. Stir in peaches, lemon juice and margarine; heat through and keep warm while topping is prepared. Biscuit Topping: Stir together flour, sugar, baking powder and salt. Cut in margarine until mixture resembles coarse crumbs. Combine egg and milk; add all at once to flour mixture. Stir just to moisten. Turn hot filling into a greased 1 ½ quart or 2 quart casserole. Immediately spoon on topping in 8 mounds. Bake approximately 20 minutes.

"This recipe also works well with 4 cups fresh berries. I've tried both raspberries and blackberries with success. It makes a great summertime treat."

Maggy Flath   **Nevada Union High School, Grass Valley, CA**

Pineapple Brown Sugar Crisp

Serves 6 - 8

1 large pineapple, about 4 pounds, cut into 1" chunks
¼ cup sugar
1 tablespoon quick tapioca
1 cup flour
1 cup light brown sugar
½ cup unsalted butter, cold, cut into pieces

Preheat oven to 375 degrees. Put pineapple into a deep, 2 quart baking dish. Sprinkle with sugar and tapioca. Toss to mix. In medium bowl, mix flour and brown sugar until blended. Add butter, cutting in with pastry blender until crumbly. Sprinkle over pineapple. Bake 40 minutes or until bubbly on top, brown and crisp. Cool.

"The tapioca in this recipe makes the juice nice and thick and rich. No more runny desserts!"
Delaine Smith   **West Valley High School, Cottonwood, CA**

Strawberry-Rhubarb Crumble

Serves 6

4 cups fresh rhubarb, sliced OR 1 (20 ounce) package frozen rhubarb, thawed
3 cups strawberries, halved
½ cup sugar
1 ½ tablespoons cornstarch
1 tablespoon fresh lemon juice
Topping:
8 tablespoons butter, softened
⅓ cup almond paste, firmly packed (½ of 7 ounce package)
⅓ cup sugar
1 cup flour

Preheat oven to 400 degrees. Mix rhubarb, strawberries, sugar, cornstarch and lemon juice in large bowl; toss well to coat. Pour into 8" x 8" greased dish. Topping: Mix butter, almond paste and sugar in processor until well blended. Transfer to medium bowl. Add flour. Using fingertips, work flour into butter mixture until moist clumps form. Sprinkle topping over fruit and bake until bubbly and golden. Serve warm.

"This is a favorite recipe made by my students and served in Cafe 103,
our student-run restaurant."

Jan Hirth   **Saddleback High School, Santa Ana, CA**

Pies and Pastries

4th of July Pie

Serves 6 - 8

1 deep (9") pie shell, baked
Glaze:
4 tablespoons cornstarch
1 ¼ cups sugar
3 cups strawberries, crushed
1 tablespoon lemon juice
Filling:
¾ pint fresh blueberries
½ pint fresh red raspberries
½ pint fresh boysenberries or blackberries
1 pint fresh strawberries, sliced in half lengthwise
Garnish: whipped cream

Glaze: Thoroughly mix cornstarch with sugar; add crushed strawberries and cook over medium heat, stirring constantly, until mixture is so thick it sticks to an inverted spoon. Stir in lemon juice and cool until lukewarm. Spread a thin layer of glaze on the bottom of baked pie shell. Spread blueberries evenly over bottom. Spoon 3 or 4 tablespoons glaze over blueberries, spreading evenly. Repeat with raspberries, glaze, boysenberries, glaze, then strawberries, cut side down, on top. Brush the tops of strawberries with remaining glaze. Chill pie. Serve with a piping of whipped cream along crust edge.

"I named this dish for Independence Day for two reasons: on Fourth of July, a bounty of fresh berries of all kinds are usually available; and with piping of whipped cream, this becomes a "red, white and blue" dessert, perfect for finishing a holiday barbecue."

Ramona Anderson   **Mira Mesa High School, San Diego, CA**

Apple Sour Cream Streusel Pie

Serves 8

Streusel Topping:
⅓ cup sugar
¼ cup brown sugar
½ cup + 2 tablespoons flour
2 teaspoons cinnamon
¼ pound butter, cold
½ cup walnuts, coarsely chopped
Filling:
¾ cup sugar
2 tablespoons flour
3 eggs
1 ½ cups sour cream
1 teaspoon cinnamon
1 ½ teaspoons vanilla extract
¼ teaspoon lemon rind, grated
¼ teaspoon nutmeg
¼ teaspoon salt
4 cups tart apples, peeled, thinly sliced (Granny Smiths or Macintosh work well)
1 pastry pie shell

Streusel Topping: Combine sugars, flour and cinnamon. Cut in butter until crumbly. Toss with walnuts. Refrigerate to keep butter from melting into dough. Filling: Preheat oven to 350 degrees. Blend together sugar, flour and eggs. Whisk in sour cream, cinnamon, vanilla, lemon rind, nutmeg and salt. Fold in apple slices. Turn into prepared pie shell. Bake on bottom shelf of oven for 20 minutes. Remove pie from oven and distribute Streusel Topping over top. Return to oven and bake 25 to 30 minutes more or until topping is crisp and browned. Let cool completely before cutting and serving.

"My sister gave me this recipe. It is her favorite pie recipe and now it's mine too!"
Terri Gravison   **Las Plumas High School, Oroville, CA**

Apple Turnovers

Serves 4 - 6

Pastry:
1 ½ cups flour, sifted
1 teaspoon salt
1 teaspoon baking powder
½ cup shortening
¼ cup ice cold water
Filling:
2 ½ cups cooked apples, pared and sliced (reserve juice)
1 cup juice (from cooked apples, add water if necessary)
½ cup sugar
2 tablespoons cornstarch
Glaze:
1 cup powdered sugar
¾ teaspoon vanilla
1 to 2 tablespoons water or milk

Pastry: Sift flour to measure 1 ½ cups; sift again with salt and baking powder. Cut in shortening with pastry blender. Mixture should be well blended and look like coarse meal. Add water in small amounts. Stir in enough water to hold the pastry dough together with a fork. Knead lightly to mix well. Sprinkle cutting board lightly with flour. Roll out pastry with rolling pin to about ⅛" thickness. Cut into 4" squares or circles. Filling: Preheat oven to 425 degrees. Mix cooled juice, sugar and cornstarch slowly, and thoroughly. Cook over medium heat, stirring often until thickened. Cool until just warm; add apples. Spoon on to pastry, about one heaping tablespoon filling per pastry. Fold over, seal edges with fork. Slit top pastry to allow steam to escape. Place on ungreased baking sheet. Bake about 10 minutes, until golden brown and filling bubbles a bit. Glaze: Stir together powdered sugar, vanilla and water or milk, 1 tablespoon at a time until smooth and shiny. Brush on with a pastry brush.

NOTE: If you want a brown crust instead of glaze, sprinkle top crust with milk and sprinkle with sugar just before baking.

"These are light, flaky and delicious."

Judi Topp   **A.B. Miller High School, Fontana, CA**

Banana Caramel Chocolate Tart

Serves 8 - 10

    Ready made pie crust
    4 bananas, sliced
    1 ounce semi-sweet chocolate, melted
    ¼ cup caramel sauce, melted
    1(4 serving) package vanilla pudding
    1 cup milk
    ½ cup nuts, chopped
    1 (small) carton Cool Whip

Bake pie crust in large tart pan following package directions for 1 crust; cool. Melt chocolate (reserve a few chips for garnishing) and cover bottom and sides of crust; let set. Cover chocolate with melted caramel sauce (reserve small amount caramel for garnish). Mix pudding with 1 cup milk; allow to set. Mix pudding with Cool Whip and sliced bananas. Pour over caramel layer. Decorate with remaining chocolate chips and nuts; drizzle with caramel sauce.

"This can be made only one day ahead. Any longer and the crust becomes soggy."

Joan Fabregue   **West High School, Torrance, CA**

Brownie Pie

Serves 6 - 8

    2 eggs
    1 cup sugar
    ½ cup butter or margarine, melted
    ½ cup flour
    ⅓ cup cocoa
    ¼ teaspoon salt
    ½ cup chocolate chips
    ½ cup nuts, chopped
    1 teaspoon vanilla

Preheat oven to 350 degrees. Grease an 8" pie plate. In small bowl, beat eggs; blend in sugar and butter. In separate bowl, stir together flour, cocoa and salt. Add to egg mixture, beating until blended. Stir in chocolate chips, nuts and vanilla. Spread into pie plate.

Bake 35 minutes or until set. (Pie will not test done in center) Cut into wedges. Top with ice cream and chocolate topping.

"We love Brownie Pie warm. It's sure to please any chocolate lover."

Kathy Arthur   **La Sierra High School, Riverside, CA**

Buttermilk Pie

Serves 6 - 8

    1 (9") pie shell
    ½ cup butter (not margarine)
    2 cups sugar
    3 rounded tablespoons flour
    3 eggs, beaten
    1 cup buttermilk
    2 teaspoons vanilla
    1 tablespoon nutmeg
    ½ cup coconut (optional)
    ½ cup nuts, chopped (optional)

Preheat oven to 350 degrees. Cream butter and sugar; add flour and eggs. Stir in buttermilk, vanilla, nutmeg, coconut and nuts. Pour into unbaked pie shell. Bake 45 to 50 minutes, until golden brown.

"This was given to me for the Youth Usher Annual Bake Sale from my friend,
Connie Garrett. It is truly delicious."

Darlene V. Brown   **Golden Valley Middle School, San Bernardino, CA**

Calypso Pie

Serves 24

    30 Oreo cookies
    ¼ cup margarine, melted
    ½ gallon vanilla ice cream, softened
    1 ½ squares unsweetened chocolate
    ⅔ cup sugar
    ⅔ cup evaporated milk
    1 tablespoon vanilla
    Pinch salt
    Garnish: whipped cream, cherries

In a ziploc bag, crush cookies, 10 at a time. Melt margarine in a 13" x 9" pan. Press crumbs in pan and freeze. Spread softened ice cream over cookies; freeze. Melt chocolate with sugar, evaporated milk, vanilla and salt. Cook 4 to 5 minutes or until it starts to thicken; cool slightly. Pour over ice cream and sprinkle with nuts. Cover and freeze. To serve, cut into squares and top with whipped cream and a cherry.

Ellen Clizbe   **Norte Vista High School, Riverside, CA**

Cannoli

Makes 10

Pastry Dough:
1 ¾ cups flour
½ teaspoon salt
2 tablespoons sugar
1 egg
2 tablespoons butter, firm
¼ cup sherry or dry sauterne wine
1 egg white
cooking oil for deep frying
Filling:
½ pound ricotta cheese
¾ cup powdered sugar
1 teaspoon vanilla
⅛ cup chocolate, chopped, semi-sweet or milk
½ cup whipping cream, whipped

Pastry: Sift flour with salt and sugar. Make a well in center; add egg and butter. Stir with a fork, working from the center out. Add wine, a little at a time, until dough comes together. Use hands to form a dough ball. Roll dough out on a floured board about 1/16" thick. Cut into approximately 3 ½" circles. Roll into ovals, wrap dough around an aluminum cannoli shell form. Seal the edges with an egg white. Fry 2 or 3 at a time, in deep fat for about 1 minute, or until lightly browned. Drain, slip off form, cool. Filling: Whirl ricotta cheese in food processor or blender until smooth. Fold in powdered sugar and vanilla. Mix in chocolate. Fold in whipping cream; chill. Using a pastry bag, fill cannoli shells. Dip each end of cannoli into chopped chocolate after filling; chill.

"Yummy - my students love these. I even have had former students come back to get the recipe!"
Beverly Fincher-Ranger   **Carpinteria High School, Carpinteria, CA**

Carolina Pecan Pie

Serves 6

¼ cup margarine, softened
½ cup brown sugar
½ cup sugar
¾ cup light corn syrup
¾ cup dark corn syrup
3 medium eggs, lightly beaten
1 teaspoon vanilla extract
1 teaspoon rum extract
¼ teaspoon brandy
2 teaspoons cornstarch
Dash salt
2 cups pecan halves (reserve best for top)
1 (9") pie crust, prepared with fluted edges

Preheat oven to 425 degrees. Cream together margarine, sugars and syrups. Beat in eggs, vanilla, rum and brandy extracts. Add cornstarch and salt. Beat 2 to 3 minutes more. Coarsely chop half of the pecans and sprinkle in bottom of pie crust. Pour filling over nuts and top with remaining pecans halves in a circular design. Wrap edges of pie crust with foil and bake

15 minutes at 425 degrees. Then, lower temperature to 275 degrees and bake 45 to 75 minutes more, or until toothpick inserted in center comes out clean.

"This is a great family favorite for gatherings."

Jannie Parks   **Ramona High School, Riverside, CA**

Cherry Lemon Pie

Serves 6 - 8

1 can lowfat Eagle Brand milk
Juice of 3 lemons OR 3 tablespoons lemon juice
3 eggs, separated
1 can sour pitted cherries, drained
2 teaspoons sugar, for meringue
1 graham cracker crust , prepared

Preheat oven to 400 degrees. In a bowl, mix Eagle brand milk with lemon juice. Add egg yolks and mix well. Fold in cherries then pour into prepared pie crust. Using mixer, beat egg whites until they form high peaks, adding sugar midway through beating. Spread meringue over top of pie and bake 15 minutes, or until tips of meringue peaks are browned. Cool on rack. Refrigerate overnight. Serve cold.

"This was my mother, Lillie Mae Lynch's, original recipe and has stood the test of time. I always receive rave reviews whenever I prepare this pie. She died October 15, 1995
- one of the loves of my life."

Cora Lynn Woodall   **Green Valley High School, Henderson, NV**

Coffee Toffee Pie

Serves 6 - 8

½ cup butter, softened
¾ cup sugar
1 square unsweetened chocolate, melted
4 teaspoons instant coffee, divided
2 eggs
8 ounces Cool Whip
Graham cracker crust, prepared

Cream butter and sugar with an electric mixer; beat until light. Blend in melted chocolate and 2 teaspoons instant coffee. Add 1 egg. Beat 5 minutes. Add second egg. Beat additional 5 minutes. Turn into graham cracker crust. Refrigerate overnight. Before serving, fold remaining 2 teaspoons instant coffee into Cool Whip. Place over toffee filling.

"A cholesterol binge - but yummy!"

Nanci Burkhart   **Hueneme High School, Oxnard, CA**

Cream Puffs With Divine Caramel Sauce

Serves 6

Cream Puffs:
1 cup water
½ cup stick margarine or butter
1 cup all-purpose flour
4 large eggs
Cream Filling:
¾ cup heavy whipping cream
2 tablespoons granulated or powdered sugar
Caramel Sauce:
2 cups water
¾ stick margarine or butter
2 cups heavy whipping cream
1 cup light corn syrup
Pinch salt
1 teaspoon vanilla

Preheat oven to 400 degrees. Cream Puffs: Heat water and margarine or butter to rolling boil in 2 ½ quart saucepan. Stir in flour, reduce heat to low. Stir vigorously over low heat, about 1 minute, or until mixture forms a ball; remove from heat. Beat in eggs, all at once; continue beating until smooth. Drop dough by scant ¼ cupfuls about 3" apart onto ungreased cookie sheet. Bake 35 to 40 minutes or until puffed and golden. Cool away from draft. Filling: Beat heavy whipping cream and sugar in chilled bowl with electric mixer on high speed until stiff. Cut off top third of each puff and pull out any strands of soft dough. Fill puffs with cream filling; replace tops, dust with powdered sugar, cover and refrigerator until ready to serve. Caramel Sauce: Heat all sauce ingredients, except vanilla, to boiling in heavy Dutch oven over medium heat, stirring constantly. Reduce heat slightly. Boil about 30 minutes, stirring frequently, until sugar is dissolved and mixture is caramel colored. Stir in vanilla. Serve hot or warm. Store in refrigerator up to 2 months.

"Students really enjoy this decadent dessert!"

Pat Freshour   **Foothill High School, Redding, CA**

Dutch Apple Bavarian Pie

Serves 6 - 8

Crust:
1 ½ cups flour
1 ½ teaspoons sugar
¾ teaspoon salt
½ cup oil
2 tablespoons milk
Cream Filling:
1 (8 ounce) package Philadelphia Cream cheese, softened
¼ cup sugar
1 egg
½ teaspoon lemon peel, grated
½ teaspoon vanilla
⅛ teaspoon salt
Apple Filling:

5 or 6 apples, peeled, sliced
1 tablespoon lemon juice (optional)
¼ teaspoon almond extract
½ teaspoon vanilla extract
½ cup sugar
¼ cup brown sugar, firmly packed
3 tablespoons flour
¼ teaspoon salt
1 teaspoon cinnamon
½ teaspoon nutmeg
½ cup almonds, sliced
Crumb Topping:
½ cup Bisquick
⅓ cup sugar
¼ cup brown sugar, firmly packed
¼ teaspoon cinnamon
3 tablespoons butter

Preheat oven to 350 degrees. Crust: Mix flour, sugar and salt in pie plate. In separate bowl, mix oil and milk; add to flour mixture. Using your fingers, press dough into deep dish pie plate. Flute edges. Cream Filling: Beat cream cheese until smooth. Add sugar, beat until smooth. Add egg, lemon peel, vanilla and salt. Beat until smooth and creamy. Pour into uncooked pie crust. Apple Filling: Mix dry ingredients together; set aside. Add lemon juice to apples, stir to coat. Add almond and vanilla extracts; mix thoroughly. Add dry ingredient mixture, mix thoroughly. Spread evenly over cream cheese layer. Sprinkle sliced almonds over top and bake pie 45 to 50 minutes. Crumb Topping: Mix Bisquick, both sugars, cinnamon and butter. Remove pie from oven and add crumb topping. Bake another 10 to 15 minutes. Remove from oven. Allow to cool at least one hour before serving.

"This recipe won 1st place in the L.A. County Fair Kids America Apple Pie Competition. I have been a judge for the youth division for many years and have enjoyed the excitement, variety and creativity of the younger contestants. This pie is an exceptional treat."

Barbara Allen **Ayala High School, Chino Hills, CA**

Fudge Ribbon Pie

Serves 10

1 (9") pastry shell, baked
Chocolate sauce:
2 (1 ounce) squares unsweetened chocolate
1 (6 ounce) can evaporated milk
1 cup sugar
2 tablespoons margarine
1 teaspoon vanilla
Filling:
1 quart peppermint ice cream, softened
Meringue:
3 egg whites
½ teaspoon vanilla
¼ teaspoon cream of tartar
6 tablespoons sugar
¼ cup peppermint candy, crushed

In saucepan, combine chocolate and evaporated milk. Cook and stir over low heat until chocolate is melted. Stir in sugar and margarine. Cook over medium heat until thickened, 5 to 8 minutes longer, stirring occasionally, Stir in vanilla; cool. Spoon half of the ice cream into cooled pastry shell. Cover with half the cooked chocolate sauce; freeze 10 to 15 minutes. Repeat with remaining ice cream and sauce. Cover and freeze until firm. Prepare meringue by beating egg whites with vanilla and cream of tartar until soft peaks form. Gradually add sugar by tablespoons, beating until stiff and glossy peaks form. Fold 3 tablespoons of crushed candy into meringue. Remove pie from freezer. Spread meringue over chocolate layer, sealing to edge. Sprinkle top with remaining 1 tablespoon crushed candy. Place pie on old, unfinished, wooden cutting board and bake at 475 degrees for 4 to 5 minutes or until golden. Serve at once.

"Very special dessert - great to serve to friends and family during the holidays!"

Cindy Elledge   **Johansen High School, Modesto, CA**

Gram Duran's Chiffon Pumpkin Pie

Serves 8

1 deep dish pie shell, baked
1 envelope unflavored gelatin
¼ cup cold water
¾ cup light brown sugar
½ teaspoon salt
2 teaspoons cinnamon
¼ teaspoon ginger
½ teaspoon allspice
1 ⅓ cups pumpkin
3 egg yolks
½ cup milk
3 egg whites
8 to 10 tablespoons sugar

Prepare deep dish pie crust, bake and allow to cool thoroughly. In a bowl, dissolve gelatin in water; set aside. In a separate mixing bowl, using an electric mixer, combine brown sugar, salt, cinnamon, ginger, allspice, pumpkin, egg yolks and milk. Transfer mixture to a double boiler and cook until thickened, approximately 20 minutes, stirring constantly. Remove from heat; add gelatin and beat with a rotary beater. Allow to cool in refrigerator until mixture begins to set, approximately 30 to 60 minutes. Then, beat again until fluffy; set aside. Prepare meringue in separate bowl by beating egg whites until frothy. Slowly add 8 to 10 tablespoons sugar and beat until stiff and glossy. Fold pumpkin mixture and meringue together. Pour into pie shell and refrigerate. (Best if allowed to set overnight) Serve with generous amounts of Cool Whip.

"This recipe is submitted in loving memory of Mrs. Katherine Duran, "Gram Duran".
Gram Duran's recipe is a tradition among her family and was passed along to me with
a number of cherished family memories and stories by her granddaughter."

Donna Collier   **John Muir Middle School, Burbank, CA**

Grandma Urke's Famous Apple Pie

Serves 6

Crust:
2 ½ cups flour
½ teaspoon salt
¾ cup Crisco shortening
4 to 6 tablespoons ice water

Filling:
7 to 8 Pippin or Fuji apples
2 tablespoons flour
1 cup sugar
1 ½ teaspoons cinnamon
⅛ teaspoon nutmeg

Stir together flour and salt. Cut in shortening until it's the size of peas. Do not cut in beyond this point. A flaky crust needs the larger chunks of shortening . Add 4 tablespoons ice water and toss with a fork. Continue to add and toss ice water until there is no dry flour remaining. Pick up dough with floured hands and shape into a ball. DO NOT work dough with your hands. Roll out dough to ⅛ to ¼" thickness and place in pie plate. Trim excess pie dough, leaving 1" hanging over the edge. Brush water under this hanging dough and fold dough under and place around rim of pie plate. Flute edges. Pie crust is now ready to be baked.

Preheat over to 350 degrees. Slice apples very thin (⅛" to ¼" thick); set aside. Mix together dry ingredients and pour over sliced apples. (Make sure apples are not wet) Pour into prepared pie crust. Cover with top crust and flute edges. Cover fluted edges with aluminum foil to avoid burning and bake 25 minutes. Remove aluminum foil and bake 25 minutes more.

> *"The key to this recipe for pie crust is ice cold water, Crisco shortening and not over mixing the dough. Grandma Urke has shared this pie with our family for years and now we share it with all of you. Honestly, the best award-winning apple pie ever!"*

Laury Urke White   **Fallbrook High School, Fallbrook, CA**

Kentucky Pecan Pie

Serves 6 - 8

1 cup light corn syrup
1 cup brown sugar
⅓ teaspoon salt
⅓ cup butter or margarine, melted
1 teaspoon vanilla
3 eggs, slightly beaten
1 heaping cup pecan halves
1 pie shell, unbaked

Preheat oven to 350 degrees. Combine first 5 ingredients and mix well. Add beaten eggs and mix together. Add pecan halves and pour into unbaked pie shell. Bake 45 minutes.

> *"Mrs. Puryear, my master teacher, gave me this recipe when I was a student teacher. I still communicate with her after 22 years. She was a wonderful teacher for whom I have a great deal of respect and love. We all should have a master teacher like her. I now make this pie for my mom on her birthday. Thank you!"*

Brenda Burke   **Mt. Whitney High School, Visalia, CA**

Key Lime Pie

Serves 8

2 (14 ounce) cans sweetened condensed milk
2 egg yolks, beaten
¾ cup key lime juice
½ cup whipping cream, whipped
2 tablespoons sugar
1 (9") pastry or graham cracker crust pie shell, prepared

Preheat oven to 350 degrees. Combine condensed milk and beaten egg yolks; gradually add key lime juice. Fill pie shell with mixture. Bake 8 to 10 minutes. Do not allow to brown. Chill at least two hours. Whip cream with sugar and top pie before serving.

"I fell in love with this pie on a Royal Caribbean cruise."

Pat Hufnagel   **Esperanza High School, Anaheim, CA**

Lemonade Pie

Serves 6 - 8

1 (12 ounce) container non-dairy topping
1 can sweetened condensed milk
1 small can frozen limeade or lemonade
1 graham cracker crust

Mix above ingredients and pour into prepared graham cracker crust. Refrigerate 1 hour.

Sherrie Miles   **Cimarron-Memorial High School, Las Vegas, NV**

Lime Angel Pie

Serves 8 - 10

Meringue Shell:
4 egg whites
¼ teaspoon cream of tartar
1 cup sugar
Dash salt
Filling:
4 egg yolks
¼ teaspoon salt
½ cup sugar
⅓ cup lime juice
Green food color
1 tablespoon lime peel, grated
2 cups whipping cream

Meringue Shell: Bring egg whites to room temperature. Add cream of tartar and beat until frothy. Gradually add sugar and salt and continue beating whites until stiff and glossy. Spread into lightly greased 9" pie plate, making depression in center with back of spoon for shell shape. Bake at 275 degrees for 20 minutes, then increase temperature to 300 degrees and bake 40 minutes longer; cool. Filling: Beat egg yolks well in top of double boiler. Beat in salt, sugar and lime juice. Cook over hot, not boiling water 10 minutes, or until thickened; cool. Tint pale green with food color. Stir in peel. Whip 1 cup cream until stiff and fold into lime mixture. Spread mixture into baked meringue shell. Whip remaining 1 cup cream, sweetened and spread over filling. Chill at least 4 hours before serving. Garnish with lime slices, if desired.

"This heavenly, refreshing pie makes a great summertime
dessert and is well worth the time and effort."

Sally Reimers   **Valley View Middle School, Simi Valley, CA**

Louisiana Pie

Serves 6 - 8

Filling:
1 (16 ounce) can yams
¼ cup brown sugar
2 tablespoons sugar
1 egg, beaten
2 teaspoons heavy cream
1 tablespoon sweet butter, softened
1 tablespoon rum extract
¼ teaspoon salt
¼ teaspoon cinnamon
¼ teaspoon nutmeg
Syrup:
¾ cup sugar
1 tablespoon butter, melted
¾ cup Karo syrup
2 eggs,
2 teaspoons rum extract
Dash salt
Dash cinnamon
¾ cup pecan pieces
Crust:
1 prepared pie crust
Garnish: whipped cream or ice cream

Preheat oven to 325 degrees. Filling: Combine ingredients until blended; set aside. Syrup: Combine all ingredients for syrup, except pecans. Beat until smooth; add pecan pieces. Pour filling into prepared pie crust and top with syrup. Bake until toothpick inserted in center comes out clean. Cool at room temperature for 24 hours.

"Serve with whipped cream or ice cream."

Edna O'Neal   **Durango High School, Las Vegas, NV**

Mini-Cherry Turnovers

Makes 10 - 12

1 ⅓ cups flour
½ teaspoon salt
½ cup shortening
3 to 4 tablespoons ice water
¼ cup cherry pie filling

Preheat oven to 475 degrees. Combine flour and salt in large mixing bowl. Cut shortening into flour and salt until particles are size of peas. Sprinkle in water, 1 tablespoon at a time, tossing with fork until all flour particles are moistened and pastry cleans sides of bowl. Gather pastry into a ball, flattened on lightly floured pastry board. Roll dough to ⅛" thickness. Using inverted small Pyrex dish, cut circles for tarts. Place 1 tablespoon cherry pie filling in each circle. Fold and press edges of dough together with fork. Cut 3 slits in upper half of circle for steam to escape. Bake 10 to 12 minutes.

"Very tasty and quick to make."

Patty Stroming   **Mitchell Sr. Elementary, Atwater, CA**

Mud Pie

Serves 12

1 package chocolate wafer cookies
¼ cup butter or margarine, melted
½ gallon coffee almond fudge or chocolate mint ice cream, softened
2 ounces unsweetened baking chocolate
1 tablespoons butter or margarine
½ cup sugar
1 (5.3 ounce) can evaporated milk
Garnish: whipped cream, toasted slivered almonds (optional)

In food processor, process cookies into fine crumbs. Add ¼ cup melted butter and process until blended. Press crumb mixture into 9" pie pan or springform pan. Freeze 10 minutes. Soften ice cream and spoon on top of crust. Freeze 30 minutes. In small saucepan, melt chocolate and 1 tablespoon butter. Add sugar and evaporated milk. Cook 5 minutes, until thick. Set aside to cool. Pour over top of pie and freeze until firm. Serve with whipped cream and slivered almonds as garnish.

"Guests love this easy to prepare dessert. May be made up to a week ahead of serving time."

Linda Falkenstien   **Morro Bay High School, Morro Bay, CA**

Peach Blitz Torte

Serves 12

4 eggs, separated
Water
1 single layer yellow cake mix (half box)
1 cup sugar
1 teaspoon vanilla
¾ cup nuts, chopped
1 cup Cool Whip
1 (1 pound 13 ounce) can sliced peaches

Preheat oven 350 degrees. To egg yolks, add enough water to make 4 ½ cup + 2 tablespoons; combine with cake mix. Pour batter into 2 greased and floured 8" cake pans. Beat egg whites, sugar and vanilla. Spread this meringue on unbaked layers. Sprinkle with nuts and bake 25 minutes. Do NOT overbake. Cool 10 minutes. Place first layer on cake plate and spread with ⅔ to ¾ of the Cool Whip. Place peach slices on top decoratively like wheel spokes (reserve some slices for center of top layer). Put top layer on and mound Cool Whip in center. Garnish with remaining peach slices. Chill thoroughly.

"This looks very dramatic when finished and tastes wonderful."

Janet Riness   **Westminster High School, Westminster, CA**

Praline Taffy Apple Pie

Serves 8

Pastry for 2 (9") pie crusts
Praline mixture:
½ cup brown sugar
½ cup pecans, chopped
⅓ cup flour
¼ cup butter, melted
Filling:
⅔ cup sugar
3 tablespoons flour
2 teaspoons cinnamon
1 teaspoon lemon juice
Dash salt
6 cups apples, sliced
11 Kraft caramels, cut in half
Half & Half

Preheat oven to 375 degrees. Lay one 9" pie crust in bottom of pie pan. Praline Mixture: In mixing bowl, combine brown sugar, pecans ⅓ cup flour and melted butter; mix well and set aside. Filling: In large mixing bowl, combine sugar, 3 tablespoons flour, cinnamon, lemon juice and dash of salt. Add apples and toss. Transfer ½ of the apple mixture to the pie shell. Top with the caramels. Repeat layer with apples and top with praline mixture. Top with remaining pie crust. Seal and flute edges. Brush crust with half & half or light cream. Cover edges with foil. Bake at 375 degrees for 25 minutes. Remove foil and bake 20 to 25 minutes more or until top is golden brown and fruit is tender. Serve warm with vanilla ice cream.

"This pie can also be made with fresh peaches...it's delicious!
This recipe comes from my sister-in-law, Tami Engel."

Adriana Molinaro   **Granite Hills High School, El Cajon, CA**

Pumpkin Nut Crumble

Serves 12

1 (18 ¼ ounce) package yellow cake mix
½ cup butter or margarine, melted
3 eggs, divided
1 (29 ounce) can pumpkin
2 teaspoons ground cinnamon
1 teaspoon ground nutmeg
1 teaspoon ground ginger
½ teaspoon ground cloves
1 cup brown sugar, packed
⅔ cup milk
Topping:
1 cup reserved cake mix
¼ cup sugar
1 teaspoon ground cinnamon
¼ cup butter or margarine, slightly softened
1 cup nuts, chopped
Garnish: Whipped cream

Preheat oven to 350 degrees. Reserve 1 cup cake mix for topping. Combine remaining cake mix, butter and 1 egg in bowl. Do not use mixer as cake mixture is crumbly, not smooth. Press mixture into bottom of greased 13" x 9" pan. In another bowl, combine pumpkin, spices, brown sugar, remaining 2 eggs and milk. Spread filling over mixture in pan. Combine topping ingredients and sprinkle over pumpkin mixture. Bake 45 to 50 minutes or until knife inserted near center comes out clean. Serve with whipped cream.

"This is especially good at Thanksgiving."

Roberta Priestley, retired   **Alhambra High School, Alhambra, CA**

Pumpkin Pie

Serves 8 - 10

Crust:
1 cup flour
1 ½ tablespoons sugar
¼ teaspoon baking powder
½ cup cold butter, minus 1 tablespoon
1 egg yolk
½ teaspoon vanilla
Filling:
2 eggs, slightly beaten
2 cups (16 ounce) pumpkin
½ cup brown sugar
2 teaspoons cinnamon
½ teaspoon nutmeg
¼ teaspoon cloves
1 (13 ounce) can evaporated milk
Garnish: whipped topping, cinnamon

Crust: Mix together flour, sugar and baking powder. Cut in cold butter with a pastry blender.

With a fork, stir in egg yolk and vanilla; mix well. Pat into bottom and up sides of a pie pan. Filling: Preheat oven to 425 degrees. Combine eggs, pumpkin, brown sugar, cinnamon, nutmeg and cloves, mixing well. Stir in evaporated milk. Pour into pie shell. Cover edge of crust with foil. Bake 15 minutes at 425 degrees, then reduce temperature to 350 degrees and bake 45 minutes, or until middle is set. Cool. Garnish with whipped topping and sprinkle with cinnamon.

Becky Oppen   **Dana Hills High School, Dana Point, CA**

Raspberry Delight
Serves 10 - 12

Crust:
1 ¼ cups graham cracker crumbs
¼ cup butter, melted
¼ cup pecans, chopped
Filling:
50 marshmallows
1 cup milk
1 pint whipped cream, whipped OR 2 cartons Cool Whip
Topping:
2 (10 ounce) packages frozen raspberries OR 2 cans raspberry pie filling
1 cup water
2 teaspoons lemon juice
4 tablespoons cornstarch dissolved in ¼ cup cold water

Crust: Combine ingredients and press into a 9" x 15" pan. Filling: In a double boiler, melt marshmallows with milk; cool completely. Fold in whipped cream and refrigerate 1 hour. Pour filling into prepared pan and refrigerate again. Topping: In large saucepan, combine raspberries, 1 cup water, and lemon juice; bring to a boil, then add cornstarch dissolved in water. Stir until thickened. Cool completely at room temperature. Pour over filling and serve.

Eloise Hatfield   **Poston Junior High School, Mesa, AZ**

Red Letter Day Torte
Serves 9 - 12

Crust:
2 cups flour
1 teaspoon salt
1 cup shortening
1 egg
Filling:
1 (16 ounce) can pitted tart red cherries, water packed (reserve juice)
Water + reserved cherry juice to equal 1 cup
¾ cup sugar
3 egg yolks, slightly beaten (reserve whites)
3 tablespoons quick-cooking tapioca
2 teaspoons red food coloring
2 teaspoons lemon juice
Meringue:
3 egg whites
1 teaspoon vanilla
¼ teaspoon cream of tartar

121

Dash salt
¾ cup sugar
1 cup walnuts, chopped

Preheat oven to 425 degrees. Crust: Sift flour and salt. Cut in shortening. Stir in slightly beaten egg until soft dough forms. Pat over bottom of baking dish. Bake approximately 20 minutes, or until lightly browned. Remove from oven and reduce heat to 350 degrees. Filling: Combine cherry juice with water (to equal 1 cup), sugar, egg yolks, tapioca and red food color in saucepan; let stand 5 minutes. Cook and stir over low to medium heat until mixture thickens and comes to a boil. Stir in cherries and lemon juice. While mixture cools, prepare meringue: beat egg whites with vanilla, cream of tartar and dash of salt until soft peaks form. Slowly add sugar, beating to stiff peaks. Fold in chopped nuts. Pour filling over baked crust; top filling with meringue, sealing edges. Bake about 20 minutes, or until lightly browned. Cool.

"Absolutely yummy!"

Roberta Hawkes   **A.B. Miller High School, Fontana, CA**

Rhubarb Custard Pie

Serves 6 - 8
3 eggs, slightly beaten
2 ⅔ tablespoons milk
2 cups sugar
¾ teaspoon nutmeg
2 (10") pie crusts
4 cups rhubarb (about 9 good stalks)
1 tablespoon butter

Preheat oven to 400 degrees. Beat eggs slightly with milk. Mix in sugar and nutmeg. Add rhubarb and stir. Place mixture into pastry lined pan and dot with butter. Cover with lattice pastry top. Bake 50 to 60 minutes. Cover crust the last 15 minutes with tin foil to prevent burning.

"Thanks to my best friend, Jane, from Wisconsin for this delicious recipe!"

Ruth Anne Mills   **Los Alisos Intermediate School, Mission Viejo, CA**

Strawberry Cream Cheese Pie

Serves 6
3 ounces cream cheese
2 tablespoons powdered sugar
6 cups fresh strawberries
1 cup sugar
3 tablespoons cornstarch
½ cup water
1 pie shell (frozen or homemade)

Beat cream cheese with powdered sugar. Spread over bottom of cooled pie crust. Cut off stems and put strawberries upside down over cream cheese mixture. Blend enough strawberries in blender to make 1 cup. Combine blended strawberries with sugar and cornstarch in saucepan. Gradually add water and stir. Cover over medium heat until mixture thickens and bubbles for 1 minute. Cool. Pour over strawberries in pie shell and chill 3 hours.

"My sister gave me this recipe, and it makes a beautiful summer treat."

Sue Campbell   **Chico Junior High School, Chico, CA**

Strawberry Pizza

Serves 5 - 6

Crust:
1 cup flour
1 stick margarine
¼ cup powdered sugar
Cream cheese layer:
½ cup sugar
1 (8 ounce) package cream cheese
Topping:
1 cup strawberry nectar
¼ cup sugar
4 teaspoons cornstarch
2 pints strawberries, sliced
Red food coloring (optional)

Preheat oven to 325 degrees. Crust: Mix flour, margarine and sugar in a bowl until mixture forms a stiff dough. Pat onto pizza pan to within 1" of edge of pan. Bake 15 to 20 minutes; cool. Cream cheese layer: Cream sugar and cream cheese together in medium bowl. Spread on cooled crust. Topping: Combine strawberry nectar, sugar and cornstarch in a saucepan. Cook on medium heat until thickened, about 15 to 20 minutes, stirring constantly. Add red food coloring at this point, if desired. Cool nectar mixture; stir in berries and spread on crust. Chill.

"Our foods classes prepare this when we study our fruits unit."

Diane Castro **Temecula Valley High School, Temecula, CA**

Sweet Potato Pie

Serves 6 - 8

3 small sweet potatoes
1 stick butter
2 cups sugar
3 eggs
1 teaspoon vanilla
1 teaspoon nutmeg
½ teaspoon cinnamon
1 cup cream
1 pie shell, unbaked

Preheat oven to 400 degrees. Boil sweet potatoes, drain, peel, and mash. Add remaining ingredients and mix well. Pour into prepared pie shell. Bake 50 minutes, or until firm.

"This recipe was very popular at our annual Black Student Union Luncheon. It was originally from Emma Austin, mother of Isaac "Ike" Austin, former LPHS basketball player, currently signed on with the L.A. Clippers."

Terri Gravison **Las Plumas High School, Oroville, CA**

Toll House Pie

Serves 6 - 8

    2 eggs
    ½ cup flour
    ½ cup sugar
    ½ cup brown sugar, firmly packed
    1 cup butter, melted and cooled to room temperature
    1 (6 ounce) package Nestlé Toll House semi-sweet chocolate morsels
    1 cup walnuts, chopped
    1 (9") pie shell, unbaked
    Whipped cream or ice cream (optional)

Preheat oven to 325 degrees. In large bowl, beat eggs until foamy. Add flour, sugar and brown sugar; beat until well blended. Blend in butter. Stir in chocolate morsels and nuts. Pour into pie shell. Bake 1 hour. Remove from oven. Serve warm with whipped cream or ice cream.

NOTE: Recipe may be doubled. Bake 2 pies... freeze one for later!

"If you like Toll House cookies, you'll LOVE this recipe!"

Carole Delap   **Golden West High School, Visalia, CA**

Apple Bread Pudding With Vanilla Custard Sauce

Serves 8

Pudding:
1 cup brown sugar
2 eggs, beaten
2 cups milk
½ teaspoon cinnamon
2 teaspoons vanilla
4 cups day old white or French bread or rolls, torn into pieces
4 cups apples, thinly sliced, chopped
Vanilla Custard Sauce:
3 egg yolks
¾ cup sugar
¼ cup cornstarch
3 cups milk
2 teaspoons vanilla

Preheat oven to 350 degrees. Combine brown sugar, eggs, milk, cinnamon and vanilla in large bowl. Add bread and apples; mix well. Pour into greased 9" x 9" square baking pan. Bake 50 minutes, or until apples are tender. Serve warm or chilled with Vanilla Custard Sauce. Sauce: Combine yolks, sugar and cornstarch in top of double boiler. Gradually add milk, stirring until smooth. Cook, over boiling water, stirring constantly until mixture thickens and coats a metal spoon. Remove from heat and stir in vanilla.

Sharon Turner   **El Dorado High School, Placentia, CA**

Apricot Pudding

Serves 12

2 (1 pound 14 ounce) cans apricot halves
½ cup sugar
¼ cup almonds, chopped
1 package yellow cake mix
½ pound butter or margarine, melted

Preheat oven to 350 degrees. Drain apricots, reserving juice from one can. Add sugar to syrup and heat to boiling. Arrange apricots in a 9" x 13" pan. Pour syrup over apricots. Sprinkle almonds over apricots. Sprinkle dry cake mix evenly over apricots and pour melted margarine or butter over cake mix. Bake 25 to 35 minutes, or until top is golden brown. Serve warm or cold with or without whipped cream or ice cream.

"A former neighbor, who died of Alzheimer's disease, many years ago, shared this recipe with me. She was a dynamite cook. Every time I serve it, I have wonderful memories of our friendship."
Charla Rayl   **Fallbrook High School, Fallbrook, CA**

Chocolate Curl Mousse

Serves 14
> 8 ounces semi-sweet chocolate, cut up
> 7 tablespoons strong coffee
> 2 tablespoons rum (optional)
> 5 eggs, separated
> 2 ounces sweet butter
> 1 cup heavy cream, whipped
> 24 ladyfingers
> *Garnish*: whipped cream, chocolate curls, maraschino cherries, with stems

Put chocolate and coffee in heavy saucepan over low heat; stir until dissolved, then add rum. Remove from heat. Add egg yolks, one at a time, stirring constantly. Add butter, bit by bit. Add whipped heavy cream to chocolate mixture. In separate bowl, beat egg whites until stiff. Slowly fold egg whites into chocolate mixture. Lightly butter a 10" springform pan and line with split ladyfingers. Fill with mousse and chill in the freezer overnight. Remove and take off spring pan sides. Garnish as desired, with whipped cream and lots of chocolate curls and a cherry in the middle.

"What more could a dessert lover ask for?"
Betty Byrne   **Vaca Pena Middle School, Vacaville, CA**

Chocolate Trifle

Serves 8 - 12
> 1 box chocolate cake mix, prepared
> 1 large box instant chocolate pudding mix, prepared
> 1 large container Cool Whip
> 6 Skor candy bars, crushed

Prepare cake as directed on package, using a 13" x 9" pan. Cool and cut into 1" x 1" squares. Make instant pudding according to package directions. Using a large glass bowl, layer ingredients: 1 layer cake cubes, layer of pudding, layer of Cool Whip, layer of crushed candy; repeat until ingredients are used up. Decorate top of truffle with crushed peppermint sticks, if desired. Mint leaves will work as well.

Jennifer Walker   **Bloomington High School, Bloomington, CA**

Cranberry Bread Pudding

Serves 6 - 8

4 cups stale French or Italian bread, buttered and cut into cubes
1 teaspoon cinnamon
1 cup dried cranberries
5 tablespoons Grand Marnier
5 eggs
2 cups milk
½ teaspoon salt
½ cup sugar
¼ cup brown sugar
1 teaspoon vanilla

Preheat oven to 350 degrees. Spray with nonstick cooking spray or grease a casserole dish. Butter and cube bread to make 4 cups. Put bread in casserole and sprinkle with cinnamon. In small dish, combine cranberries and Grand Marnier; microwave on HIGH for 1 minute. In another bowl, beat remaining ingredients. Sprinkle bread cubes with cranberries and any remaining liquid. Cover with egg and milk mixture. Push bread under surface of liquid. Bake 55 minutes, or until knife inserted in center comes out clean.

"I serve this with sweetened whipped cream with a bit more Grand Marnier.
Dried cherries are nice too!"

Lynda Ruth   **La Mirada High School, La Mirada, CA**

Danish Rice Pudding

Serves 8

2 cups rice, cooked
2 cups milk
⅓ cup sugar
1 teaspoon almond extract
1 cup heavy cream
1 (10 ounce) package frozen sweetened raspberries, thawed
8 whole almonds

Heat rice, milk and sugar in 2 quart saucepan over medium heat, stirring frequently until pudding is thick and creamy, about 15 minutes. Do not boil. Remove from heat; add almond extract; cool. Beat cream in chilled bowl until stiff peaks form. Fold whipped cream into cooled rice mixture. Blend raspberries in blender until smooth; strain. To serve, place pudding in custard cups. Dollop with 1 tablespoon raspberry sauce and top with almond.

USA Rice Council   **Houston, TX**

Four Layer Refrigerator Dessert

Serves 12

1 cup flour
1 cup pecans, chopped
1 stick butter, melted
2 tablespoons sugar
1 (8 ounce) package cream cheese, softened
1 cup powdered sugar
9 ounces Cool Whip

127

1 (6 ounce) package instant chocolate pudding
3 cups milk
Garnish: grated chocolate, chopped pecans

Preheat oven to 350 degrees. Mix together flour, pecans, butter and sugar; pat into a 9" x 13" pan. Bake 15 minutes; cool. Mix cream cheese, powdered sugar and 1 cup Cool Whip. Spread over first layer. Mix pudding and milk according to package directions. Spread over second layer. Spread remaining Cool Whip over top. Top with grated chocolate and chopped pecans. Refrigerate.

"You can also use lemon or banana pudding."

Bonnie Shrock   **Kearny High School, San Diego, CA**

Karen's Hawaiian Delight

Serves 12
Crust:
1 ½ cups flour
¾ cup butter, softened
½ cup pecans, finely chopped
nonstick cooking spray
Filling:
3 large bananas
3 cups nonfat milk
2 large boxes vanilla sugar-free pudding
1 small can crushed pineapple, with juice
1 large light Cool Whip, sugar free
2 teaspoons coconut extract

Preheat oven to 350 degrees. Crust: Combine ingredients; press into 9" x 12" pan that has been sprayed with nonstick cooking spray. Bake 25 to 30 minutes; cool. Filling: Slice bananas onto cooled crust. In bowl, combine milk and vanilla pudding, mix well. Add crushed pineapple and coconut extract. Fold in ½ container of Cool Whip. Pour over bananas and crust. Top with remaining cool whip and refrigerate. Cut into squares and serve.

"Served many times at family and church gatherings. My sister, Karen, has had many compliments."

Sonja Tyree   **Ayala High School, Chino Hills, CA**

L.B.J. Dessert

Serves 8
1st layer:
1 ½ sticks butter
1 ½ cups flour
½ cup nuts, chopped
2nd layer:
1 (8 ounce) cream cheese
1 cup powdered sugar
1 cup Cool Whip
3rd layer:
1 large package instant chocolate pudding mix
2 ½ cups milk

"Lollipop" Cookies
page 142

50% Less Fat!

Brownies, page 140
Chocolate Orange Cake, page 141

Topping:
Cool Whip
Coconut
Chopped nuts

Preheat oven to 350 degrees. Mix together 1st layer and press into bottom of a 8" x 13" pan. Bake 20 minutes. Combine 2nd layer and pour over 1st layer. Combine 3rd layer and pour over 2nd layer. Top 3rd layer with Cool Whip and sprinkle with coconut and nuts. Let stand in refrigerator 8 hours or overnight.

"This is rich, delicious and there is nothing lowfat about it!
But it's okay to splurge once in awhile."

Bonnie Culp   **Montclair High School, Montclair, CA**

Marshmallow Mocha

Serves 4 - 6
20 regular marshmallows
½ cup strong black coffee, hot
½ pint whipping cream, whipped
Garnish: chocolate curls

Melt marshmallows in coffee over low heat, stirring until mixture forms a syrup; cool. Fold in whipped cream. Place in individual parfait glasses and refrigerate several hours before serving. Garnish with chocolate curls.

"Elegant, easy and delicious!"

Linda Paskins   **Cordova High School, Rancho Cordova, CA**

Old English Trifle

Serves 12
1 (4 ounce) box vanilla pudding (not instant)
2 cups half & half
2 tablespoons dark rum
2 ¼ cups whipping cream
3 tablespoons sugar
¼ cup brandy
¼ cup sherry
1 (10") round sponge cake, sliced OR 3 packages lady fingers
1 package red raspberries

Combine pudding with half & half. Cook, stirring until mixture boils and thickens. Add rum, then chill mixture. Whip 1 ¼ cups whipping cream with 2 tablespoons sugar until stiff. Fold into chilled pudding. Prepare dish with ladyfingers or sponge cake slices on sides and bottom. Combine brandy and sherry. Sprinkle sponge cake or lady fingers with about 2 tablespoons liquid; layer ⅓ of chilled pudding mixture, then raspberries; repeat two more times. Whip remaining whipping cream with 2 tablespoons sugar until stiff. Spread on top. Drizzle with remaining raspberries. Chill at least 6 hours.

"Use a glass deep bowl with straight sides."

Sally Engel   **Elsinore Middle School, Lake Elsinore, CA**

Pumpkin Dessert Dip

Serves 8 - 10

 2 cups powdered sugar
 1 (8 ounce) package fat free or light cream cheese, softened
 1 (15 ounce) can pumpkin
 1 teaspoon cinnamon
 ½ teaspoon ginger
 hollowed out pumpkin shell
 ginger snaps, vanilla wafers and/or bagels

Blend together cream cheese and powdered sugar. Add pumpkin and spices; mix well. Chill. Serve in hollowed out pumpkin shell with ginger snaps, vanilla wafers or on bagels.

"This is great on toast or bagels in the morning and just as tasty as a party dip or when playing bridge."

Sue Walters   **Morse High School, San Diego, CA**

Steamed Pudding

Serves 10

 ½ cup butter
 1 cup sugar
 2 eggs, beaten
 1 cup carrots, grated
 1 cup nuts, chopped
 1 cup dates, cup up (optional)
 1 cup flour, sifted
 1 teaspoon baking soda
 1 teaspoon cinnamon
 ½ teaspoon ground cloves
 1 teaspoon nutmeg
 1 ½ cups bread crumbs
 Sauce:
 1 cup sugar
 ¼ teaspoon cinnamon
 ¼ teaspoon nutmeg
 1 ½ tablespoons cornstarch
 1 cup water
 2 tablespoons butter
 1 tablespoon vanilla
 1 tablespoon rum extract or ¼ cup rum (optional)

Cream together butter and sugar. Add eggs and beat until light and fluffy. Stir in carrots, nuts and fruits. Sift together dry ingredients, combine with bread crumbs and stir into batter until well blended. Pour into a greased mold or container (such as wide mouth canning jars with sealing lids). Cover and steam 2 hours or until wood skewer inserted in center comes out dry. While pudding cooks, prepare sauce. Mix sugar, cinnamon, nutmeg, cornstarch thoroughly with water and butter. Stir and cook until thick and clear. Add vanilla and flavor with rum extract or rum, if desired. Serve over hot steamed pudding.

"Traditional Christmas Eve dinner dessert in my family. I looked forward to it each year as a little girl."
Sue Fullmer   **Mojave High School, N. Las Vegas, NV**

Quick Breads

A Different Banana Bread

Makes 2 loaves

- 1 cup shortening
- 2 cups sugar
- 4 eggs
- 6 ripe bananas, mashed
- 4 cups flour
- 2 teaspoons baking soda
- ½ cup chocolate chips
- ½ cup maraschino cherries, halved
- ½ cup nuts, chopped

Preheat oven to 350 degrees. Cream together shortening, sugar and eggs. Stir in bananas. Sift flour and baking soda in separate bowl. Mix into creamed mixture. Fold in chocolate chips, cherries and nuts. Pour into 2 greased and floured loaf pans. Bake 1 hour to 1 hour and 15 minutes.
"A little different banana bread - it's quite tasty!"

Monica Carlson   **La Contenta Junior High School, Yucca Valley, CA**

Apple Pancakes

Serves 2

- 2 eggs
- ½ cup milk
- 1 cup flour
- ½ teaspoon salt
- 2 teaspoons baking powder
- 1 packet Equal
- ¼ cup oil
- 1 cup apples, diced
- 1/ teaspoon cinnamon
- ½ teaspoon nutmeg

Mix together eggs and milk. Sift flour together with salt, baking powder and Equal. Add egg mixture to flour and beat until smooth. Stir in oil and apples. Stir in cinnamon and nutmeg. Cook pancakes on hot griddle.

Jackie Welch-Doubeck   **Burkholder Middle School, Henderson, NV**

Baked Apple Doughnuts

Serves 6

>   1 ½ cups presifted flour
>   1 ¾ teaspoons baking powder
>   ½ teaspoon nutmeg
>   ½ teaspoon salt
>   ½ cup sugar
>   ⅓ cup shortening
>   ¼ cup milk
>   1 egg, beaten
>   ½ cup grated apple (pippin or Granny Smith)
>   1 teaspoon cinnamon
>   ¼ cup sugar
>   ½ cup butter, melted

Preheat oven to 350 degrees. In large bowl, using pastry blender, stir together flour, baking powder, nutmeg, salt and sugar. Using pastry blender, cut in shortening. In a small bowl, combine milk and egg. Make a well in center of flour mixture and pour in egg/milk mixture and grated apple. Stir just until moistened. Do not overmix. Use paper muffin cups or grease bottoms of muffin pan. Fill cups ⅔ full of batter. Bake 20 to 25 minutes; remove from pan, then remove paper cups, if using. Combine 1 teaspoon cinnamon and ¼ cup sugar; set aside. Melt butter in microwave. Roll doughnuts in melted butter, then in cinnamon/sugar mixture. Serve warm.

"I have been using this recipe in class for about 20 years, and the students still love it."

Reiko Ikkanda   **South Pasadena Middle School, South Pasadena, CA**

Biscotti

Makes 9 dozen

>   2 cups sugar
>   1 cup butter, melted
>   ¼ cup anise seeds
>   ¼ cup anisette liqueur
>   3 tablespoons whiskey
>   6 eggs (or equivalent Egg Beaters)
>   1 tablespoon baking powder
>   5 ½ cups flour
>   2 cups walnuts or almonds, coarsely chopped

Preheat oven to 375 degrees. In large bowl, mix sugar with melted butter, anise seeds, anisette and whiskey; beat in eggs. In another bowl, mix baking powder with flour; stir thoroughly into sugar mixture. Stir in nuts. Cover and refrigerate 2 to 3 hours. Roll dough into round ropes. Lay on a cookie sheet that has been sprayed with nonstick cooking spray. Flatten ropes into ½" thick loaves, approximately 2" wide. Place loaves 3 to a cookie sheet with plenty of room between each loaf. Bake approximately 20 minutes or until lightly browned.

Remove from oven and let loaves cool on baking sheet. Then, cut each loaf into diagonal slices ½" to ¾" thick. Place slices closely together on baking sheet and bake an additional 15 minutes or until lightly toasted. Cool on wire racks and store in airtight container.

"Thanks to my friend, Jan Roach, for sharing one of her family's special recipes. It is excellent dipped in hot coffee or cocoa."

Mary Springhorn   **Anderson High School, Anderson, CA**

Buttermilk Scones with Lemon Curd

Makes 3 cups

Scones:
1 ¾ cups self rising flour
Pinch of salt
⅛ cup butter
2 tablespoons + ½ teaspoon sugar
1 egg
5 ounces buttermilk

Lemon Curd:
4 teaspoons grated lemon peel
⅔ cup lemon juice
5 eggs
1 cup sugar
½ cup butter or margarine, melted

Preheat oven to 450 degrees. Scones: Sift flour and salt together; cut in the butter until mixture looks like bread crumbs. Stir in sugar. Lightly beat egg and add to flour mixture. Add enough buttermilk to make a firm, light dough. Knead lightly. Roll out on a floured board to a thickness or ¼ to ½". Cut into 2" rounds and place on a lightly greased baking sheet. Bake 10 to 15 minutes, until golden and firm. Cool. Serve with lemon curd. Lemon Curd: In container of a blender, combine lemon peel, lemon juice, eggs and sugar; whirl until smooth. With motor at lowest speed, gradually add melted butter or margarine, pouring in a steady stream; whirl just until blended. Transfer mixture to a small heavy pan and cook over medium heat, stirring constantly, about 5 minutes, or until it begins to bubble and thickens. Remove from heat. Cool slightly, cover and refrigerate or freeze. It keeps in the refrigerator for about 1 week or in the freezer for several months.

NOTE: To make cheese scones, replace sugar with 2 ounces grated cheese.

"These are delicious and a real family favorite."

Joan Wayland   **O. W. Holmes Junior High School, Davis, CA**

Cheddar Apple Nut Bread

Makes 1 loaf

2 ½ cups flour
¾ cup sugar
2 teaspoons baking powder
½ teaspoon salt
1 teaspoon cinnamon
2 eggs, beaten
¾ cup milk
⅓ cup margarine, melted
2 cups cheddar cheese, grated
1 ½ cups apples, peeled, chopped
¾ cup walnuts, chopped

Preheat oven to 350 degrees. Combine dry ingredients. Add eggs, milk and margarine; blend well. Stir in remaining ingredients; blend well. Spoon into well greased and floured 9" x 5" loaf pan. Bake 65 to 70 minutes, or until a toothpick inserted in center comes out clean.

"Very good - perfect for a holiday brunch!"

Elizabeth DeMars   **West Hills High School, Santee, CA**

Danish Puff

Serves 4 - 6

Pastry:
½ cup butter
1 cup flour
¼ teaspoon salt
2 tablespoons cold water
Filling:
1 cup boiling water
½ cup butter
1 teaspoon almond extract
1 cup flour
3 eggs
Frosting:
1 cup powdered sugar, sifted
2 tablespoons cream
⅛ teaspoon salt
1 tablespoon butter, softened
1 teaspoon vanilla

Pastry: Cut ½ cup butter into 1 cup flour and salt. Add cold water and blend well. Divide dough in half. Pat each half into a 3" x 12" rectangle on an ungreased baking sheet; set aside. Filling: Combine boiling water and remaining ½ cup butter in saucepan. Boil until butter melts; add almond extract and remove from heat. Immediately add remaining 1 cup flour and beat until smooth. Beat in eggs, one at a time. Spread onto pastry rectangles. Frosting: Combine ingredients until smooth. Drizzle on top of pastry and filling. Bake at 425 degrees for 15 minutes, then lower heat to 400 degrees and bake 25 minutes; lower heat to 350 degrees and bake 10 minutes more. Cool before serving.

"This sounds complicated - it's not. It's delicate flavor is well worth the little effort."

Jean Hanson   **Red Bluff Union High School, Red Bluff, CA**

Kay's Date Nut Bread

Makes 1 loaf

1 ½ cups boiling water
1 cup chopped dates
2 ⅔ cups flour
2 teaspoons baking soda
¼ teaspoon salt (optional)
1 ½ cups sugar
¼ cup margarine (½ cube) softened
1 teaspoon vanilla
1 egg, beaten
1 cup pecans or walnuts, chopped
Powdered sugar

Preheat oven to 350 degrees. In small mixing bowl, pour boiling water over dates. Let stand while assembling other ingredients. Sift together flour, baking soda and salt into a bowl; stir. Add sugar, margarine, vanilla, egg, nuts and dates, including water. Mix well with an electric mixer or wooden spoon. Lightly grease a loaf pan or spray with nonstick cooking spray. Pour batter into pan and bake 1 hour and 15 minutes, or until toothpick inserted in center comes out clean. Cool in pan 20 minutes before removing. Sprinkle with powdered sugar on top when cooled.

"My mother, Kay Kingsbury, made this bread for all her friends and family at Christmas time. It is not "low fat", but it is delicious!"

Marianne L. Traw   **Ball Junior High School, Anaheim, CA**

Lemon Tea Bread

Serves 8 - 12

Lemony Glaze:
¼ cup lemon juice
½ cup sugar
Bread:
⅓ cup butter, melted
1 cup sugar
3 tablespoons lemon extract
2 eggs
1 ½ cups all purpose flour
1 teaspoon baking powder
1 teaspoon salt
½ cup milk
1 ½ tablespoons lemon peel, grated
½ cup pecans, chopped

Preheat oven to 350 degrees. Grease and flour a 9" x 5" loaf pan; set aside. Lemony Glaze: Mix lemon juice and sugar in a small bowl; set aside. Bread: In a large bowl, cream butter, sugar, and lemon extract until fluffy. Add eggs, beating until mixture is blended. In medium bowl, sift flour, baking powder and salt. Pour ⅓ of the flour mixture into egg mixture. Add ⅓ of the milk. Stir until blended. Continue adding flour and milk alternately until all is blended. Do not overmix. Fold in lemon peel and pecans. Pour batter into prepared pan. Bake 1 hour or until wooden pick inserted in center comes out clean. Remove bread from oven and immediately pour Lemony Glaze slowly over the top. Let stand 15 to 20 minute. Turn out on to rack and cool. (May be frozen.) Before serving bread, bring to room temperature. Cut in thin slices, serve with butter, if desired.

"This bread recipe was a hit at our Secretary's Day English Tea & Fashion Show. The recipe was given to us by the President of our PTA, Maureen Layton."

Debbie Thompson   **Foothill High School, Tustin, CA**

Mrs. Hughes' Cinnamon Biscuits
Makes 12

Biscuits:
⅓ cup raisins, chopped
2 cups flour
2 tablespoons sugar
1 teaspoon salt
1 teaspoon cinnamon
1 tablespoon baking powder
¼ cup butter
¼ cup shortening
¾ cup milk
Glaze:
1 cup powdered sugar
½ teaspoon vanilla
1 to 2 tablespoons milk

Preheat oven to 450 degrees. Chop raisins and soak in warm water until softened. Using a large mixing bowl, combine flour, sugar, salt, cinnamon and baking powder. Using a pastry blender, cut butter and shortening into flour mixture. The mixture should have only small lumps of butter and shortening visible. Using a wooden spoon, stir in milk until mixture comes together and cleans sides of bowl. Fold in chopped raisins. Put about ½ cup flour on the cutting board. Turn biscuit mixture onto flour and knead 10 to 12 times, adding flour to your hands as necessary. Roll dough to about 1" thickness (about the width of your thumb). (NOTE: You don't want the dough to be too thin. The dough will only double in size in the baking process. Your biscuits should be at least 2" high when finished.) Using a biscuit cutter or plastic cup, cut biscuits out by dipping the cutter into flour before cutting. Place biscuits on ungreased baking sheet. Bake 10 to 12 minutes. Glaze when cool. Glaze: Mix together powdered sugar, vanilla. add milk, 1 tablespoon at a time, stirring until smooth.

"These biscuits are so good that my students want to open a Cinnamon Biscuit Store and sell them for profit."

Sandra Hughes   **Upland High School, Upland, CA**

Pumpkin Bread
Makes 2 loaves

3 ½ cups flour, sifted
3 ½ cups sugar
2 teaspoons baking soda
1 ½ teaspoons salt
1 teaspoon cinnamon
1 teaspoon nutmeg
½ teaspoon cloves
1 cup oil
⅔ cup water
4 eggs
2 cups pumpkin
1 cup nuts, chopped

Preheat oven to 350 degrees. Sift all dry ingredients together. In another bowl, combine remaining ingredients, except nuts. Make a well in center of dry ingredients and add wet ingredients. Stir until flour is just moist. Fold in nuts. Bake 55 minutes or until done.

"Everyone's favorite at Thanksgiving!"

Sharon Chavez   **Rogers Middle School, Long Beach, CA**

Quick Pumpkin Bread

Makes 5 round loaves

- 4 cups canned pumpkin
- 4 cups sugar
- 1 cup oil
- 1 tablespoon vanilla
- 2 eggs
- 5 cups flour
- 3 teaspoons cinnamon
- 1 teaspoon cloves
- ¼ teaspoon ginger
- 1 teaspoon salt
- 1 tablespoon baking soda
- 1 cup walnuts, chopped

Preheat oven to 350 degrees. In a large bowl, combine pumpkin, sugar and oil. Add vanilla and eggs; mix well. In a medium bowl, combine flour, cinnamon, cloves, ginger, salt and baking soda. Gradually add dry ingredients to pumpkin mixture. Stir in walnuts. Grease five one pound coffee cans; fill each half full. Bake 60 minutes, or until toothpick comes out clean. Remove bread to cool.

"Great for holiday giving. Wonderful flavor and very moist."

Judy Banks   **Temecula Valley High School, Temecula, CA**

Scottish Dessert Pancakes

Serves 5

- 2 cups plain flour
- ½ cup sugar
- 1 ½ tablespoons baking powder
- 2 eggs
- ½ cup milk
- 1 ½ tablespoons oil
- Water
- *Garnish*: Devonshire or whipped cream, preserves

Mix together ingredients with wire whisk. Spray griddle with oil; heat to medium heat. Cook pancakes like American pancakes except add only enough water to mix so that pancakes remain at least ½" thick. Make 4" in diameter or less. Flip when bubbles pop. Serve at room temperature, not hot. Top with Devonshire cream or whipped cream with your favorite preserves.

"These are usually served at tea time with other miniature cakes.
They are usually eaten with fingers."

Nan Paul   **Grant Middle School, Escondido, CA**

Lighter Desserts

Applesauce Spice Cake

Serves 12   **270 Calories, 5 grams fat**

Cake:
1 spice cake mix
2 cups applesauce
6 egg whites OR ¾ cup egg substitute
1 cup raisins (optional)
Garnish: powdered sugar

Preheat oven to 350 degrees. Mix cake mix, applesauce and egg whites or egg substitute; fold in raisins, if desired. Pour batter into a 9" x 13" pan that has been prepared with non-stick cooking spray. Bake 20 to 25 minutes or until tests done. When cool, sprinkle lightly with powdered sugar.

"A great quick and light dessert that can be made in a hurry. Top with whipped topping, if desired."
Diane Heider   **Hedrick Middle School, Medford, OR**

Blueberry Crisp

Serves 6   **207 Calories, 3 grams fat**

1 (16 ounce) package frozen blueberries, unsweetened, thawed
1 tablespoon + 2 teaspoons cornstarch
1 tablespoon + 1 ½ teaspoons lemon juice
2 teaspoons water
⅛ teaspoon ground nutmeg
½ cup regular oats, uncooked
¼ cup brown sugar, firmly packed
2 tablespoons + 1 ½ teaspoons all-purpose flour
¾ teaspoon ground cinnamon
2 tablespoons margarine

Preheat oven to 375 degrees. Place blueberries in a shallow 1 quart baking dish. Combine cornstarch, lemon juice, water and nutmeg, stir well. Pour over blueberries, stirring gently to coat. Combine oats, brown sugar, flour and cinnamon in a small bowl; cut in margarine with a pastry blender until mixture resembles coarse meal. Sprinkle mixture evenly over blueberries. Bake 30 minutes, or until bubbly. Spoon into individual serving bowls and serve warm.

"Serve alone or top with whipped cream, ice cream or frozen yogurt."
Kathie Baczynski   **Mt. Carmel High School, Poway, CA**

Chocolate Chip Meringue Cookies

Makes 2 - 3 dozen　　　　　　　　　　　**119 Calories, 4 grams fat**
　　2 egg whites
　　¾ cup sugar
　　6 ounces chocolate chips

Preheat oven to 350 degrees. Beat egg whites until dry and stiff. Gradually add sugar until peaks form. Stir in chocolate chips. Place by teaspoonfuls onto greased cookie sheet. Set in oven, turn off heat. Leave overnight.

　　"This is a great recipe to bake for a potluck or gift when you have very little time and have chocolate chips in the pantry. Very light and so good!"

Judy Henry　　　　　　　　　　**Newhart Middle School, Mission Viejo, CA**

Chunky Citrus Applesauce

Serves 8　　　　　　　　　　　**414 calories, 1 fat gram**
　　6 large tart apples, unpeeled
　　¼ cup apple cider or juice
　　Zest and juice from ½ orange
　　Zest and juice from ½ lemon
　　Corn syrup or sugar, to taste
　　Garnish: whipped topping and granola, fat free

Core and chop apples into large pieces. Be sure to leave skins on. This adds a nice texture and fiber. Place apples in large glass microwave-safe dish with lid. Cover and cook on HIGH until apples are fork tender, stirring every 2 minutes. If apples are too dry, add apple cider or juice. As apples cook, mash to desired consistency. Remove from microwave and stir in zest and juice from orange and lemon. Sweeten with corn syrup or sugar if applesauce is too tart.

　　"To make a dessert, put applesauce into individual dishes with dollop of whipped topping and sprinkle with granola."

Janet Tingley　　　　　　　　　　**Atascadero High School, Atascadero, CA**

Cracker Pie

Serves 6-8　　　　　　　　　　　**221 Calories, 8 grams fat**
　　3 egg whites
　　1 cup sugar
　　14 soda crackers, coarsely crumbled
　　¾ cup nuts, slivered
　　1 teaspoon baking powder
　　1 teaspoon vanilla
　　1 cup non-dairy whipped topping

Preheat oven to 350 degrees. Beat egg whites until foamy. Add sugar, gradually, beating until stiff. Combine crackers, nuts and baking powder. Fold into egg whites. Add vanilla. Bake in a buttered pie pan 40 minutes. Cool & spread with whipped cream 2 hours before serving. Serve with berries.

　　"One of my favorite recipes from my Aunt Julie, who was also a Home Economics teacher in Upland many years ago!"

Deborah Scott-Toux　　　　　　　　　　**Eisenhower High School, Rialto, CA**

Divinity

Makes 36　　　　　　　　　　　　　　　　　　**88 Calories, 2 grams fat**

2 ½ cups sugar
½ cup light corn syrup
¾ cup water
1 egg white
Pinch salt
1 tablespoon vanilla
1 cup walnuts

Place sugar, corn syrup and water in large saucepan. Cover and boil 2 minutes. Remove cover and cook to 238 degrees on candy thermometer. Remove from heat and let rest 5 minutes. Beat egg white and salt until stiff, but not dry. Slowly pour syrup in the egg whites, beating vigorously the entire time. Flavor with vanilla and nuts. Beat until mixture looses its shine. Drop by teaspoonfuls onto waxed paper.

"For best success, make on a dry, cool day. Divinity hates humidity!"

Priscilla Burns　　　　　　　　　　　**Pleasant Valley High School, Chico, CA**

Hershey's 50% Reduced Fat Chocolate Brownies

Makes 36　　　　　　　　　　　　　　　　**100 Calories, 3 grams fat**

¾ cup Hershey's Cocoa
½ teaspoon baking soda
⅔ cup lower fat (40% oil) margarine, melted, divided
½ cup boiling water
2 cups sugar
3 egg whites
1 teaspoon vanilla
1 ⅓ cups all-purpose flour
¼ teaspoon salt
1 cup Hershey's 50% Reduced Fat Semi-Sweet Baking Chips

Heat oven to 350 degrees. Spray 13" x 9" baking pan with nonstick cooking spray. In large bowl, stir together cocoa and baking soda; stir in ⅓ cup melted margarine. Add boiling water; stir until mixture thickens. Stir in sugar, egg whites, vanilla and remaining ⅓ cup melted margarine; stir until smooth. Add flour and salt; blend completely. Stir in baking chips; pour into prepared pan. Bake 30 to 35 minutes or until brownies begin to pull away from sides of pan. Cool completely in pan on wire rack. Cut into squares.

Hershey Foods Corp.　　　　　　　　　　　　　　　　　　**Hershey, PA**

Hershey's 50% Reduced Fat Chocolate Frosting

Makes 1 cup　　　　　　　　　　　　　　　　**120 Calories, 4 grams fat**

1 cup Hershey's 50% Reduced Fat Semi-Sweet Baking Chips
1 cup powdered sugar
3 tablespoons nonfat milk

In small microwave-safe bowl, place chips. Microwave at HIGH (100%) for 45 seconds; stir until melted. Gradually add powdered sugar and milk, beating with wire whisk. If necessary, microwave at HIGH additional 30 to 45 seconds or until mixture is smooth when beaten. Spread immediately.

Hershey Foods Corp.   **Hershey, PA**

Hershey's 50% Reduced Fat Chocolate Orange Cake

Serves 15   **300 Calories, 10 grams fat**

    1 cup light brown sugar, firmly packed
    ⅔ cup lower fat (40% oil) margarine
    4 egg whites
    1 cup nonfat milk
    1 tablespoon orange juice
    2 cups all-purpose flour
    2 cups quick-cooking oats
    1 tablespoon orange peel, freshly grated
    1 teaspoon baking soda
    ½ teaspoon salt
    2 cups (12 ounce package) Hershey's 50% Reduced Fat Semi-Sweet Baking Chips

Heat oven to 350 degrees. Spray 13" x 9" x 2" baking pan with nonstick cooking spray. In large bowl, stir together brown sugar, margarine and egg whites; stir in nonfat milk and orange juice. Stir in flour, oats, orange peel, baking soda, salt and chocolate chips. Spread in prepared pan. Bake 25 to 30 minutes or until light golden brown and center feels firm when touched lightly. Cool completely.

Hershey Foods Corp.   **Hershey, PA**

Joan's Ambrosia

Serves 5 - 6   **74 Calories, 0 grams fat**

    1 small box jello, any flavor desired
    1 large can fruit cocktail, well drained
    1 large Cool Whip

Sprinkle dry jello mix over drained fruit cocktail. Fold in Cool Whip; mix well. Place in serving dish and chill 2 to 3 hours.

"This is my sister's recipe. She says this is very quick and refreshing."

Margaret McLeod   **Nogales High School, La Puente, CA**

Lemon Bisque

Serves 15 - 17   **265 Calories, 9 grams fat**

    1 (13 ounce) can evaporated milk
    1 package lemon gelatin
    1 ½ cups boiling water
    ⅓ cup honey
    ⅛ teaspoon salt
    3 tablespoons lemon juice
    lemon rind, grated (from 1 lemon)
    2 ½ cups vanilla wafer crumbs

Thoroughly chill one can of milk in cracked ice or refrigerate overnight. Dissolve gelatin in boiling water; add honey, salt, lemon juice and rind. When mixture congeals slightly, beat milk until it is stiff and beat gelatin into milk mixture. Pour cookie crumbs into 9" x 13" pan. Pour mixture over crumbs and refrigerate about 3 hours. Serve plain or with whipped cream.

"To reduce calories, use lowfat products and/or sugar free jello."

Joan Fabregue   **West High School, Torrance, CA**

Lemon Granita

Serves 4 - 6   **102 Calories, 0 grams fat**

    ¾ cup sugar
    1 teaspoon lemon peel, grated
    3 cups water
    ½ cup fresh lemon juice

Place a 13" x 9" metal pan in freezer to chill. Meanwhile, in medium bowl, combine all ingredients and mix well. Pour into chilled pan. Place in freezer 30 minutes. When ice crystals begin to form at edges of pan, stir mixture with fork. Return to freezer, freeze about 2 hours or until completely frozen, stirring every 30 minutes. To serve, scoop into individual bowls.

"Our classes made this dessert during "Pasta Week", and it was a huge hit. Very light and refreshing."

Armida Gordon   **Fountain Valley High School, Fountain Valley, CA**

Lite Creme Brulee

Serves 4   **152 Calories, 2 grams fat**

    2 cups fresh raspberries
    3 tablespoons sugar
    1 tablespoon cornstarch
    1 ½ cups nonfat milk
    1 egg, slightly beaten
    3 tablespoons nonfat sour cream
    ¾ teaspoon vanilla extract
    2 tablespoons brown sugar

Line the bottom of 4 ovenproof dishes with raspberries. Combine sugar and cornstarch in saucepan. In small bowl, combine milk and egg; mix well and add to dry ingredients. Cook over medium heat, stirring constantly until boiling. Remove from heat. Let cool 5 minutes. Stir in sour cream and vanilla. Spoon custard mixture over raspberries. Place dishes on cookie sheet and sprinkle each with brown sugar. Broil 2 minutes at about 6" from heat. Serve immediately.

"I'm on a quest to find the best creme brulee. Although this one is not the winner, for 152 calories, it's pretty good!"

Jan Schulenburg   **Irvine High School, Irvine, CA**

Lollipop Cookies

Makes 24   **128 Calories, 4 grams fat**

    2 extra-ripe, medium DOLE Bananas
    ¾ cup light margarine
    ¾ cup brown sugar, firmly packed
    1 egg
    ½ teaspoon vanilla extract
    1 ½ cups quick-cooking oats
    1 ½ cups all-purpose flour

1 teaspoon ground cinnamon
½ teaspoon baking soda
½ teaspoon salt
1 ½ cups DOLE Seedless Raisins
Nonstick cooking spray
24 large wooden sticks (optional)

Purée bananas in blender. Beat margarine and sugar. Beat in egg, then puréed bananas and vanilla. Combine oats, flour, cinnamon, baking soda and salt; stir into banana mixture just until blended. Stir in raisins. Drop by rounded tablespoonfuls 2" apart on baking sheets sprayed with nonstick cooking spray. Flatten tops with back of spoon. Insert wooden stick in each cookie to resemble lollipop, if desired. Bake 12 to 15 minutes or until lightly browned; cool.

Dole Foods   **San Francisco, CA**

Lowfat Banana Muffins

Makes 16   **172 Calories, 4 grams fat**

2 cups all purpose flour
1 teaspoon baking powder
1 teaspoon baking soda
¼ teaspoon salt
3 tablespoons butter or margarine
2 eggs
¼ cup nonfat milk
2 teaspoons vanilla
½ cup sugar
2 tablespoons plain nonfat yogurt
⅓ cup applesauce
2 large bananas, mashed

Preheat oven to 375 degrees. Combine flour, baking powder, soda and salt; cut in butter or margarine. In another bowl, beat eggs; add milk, vanilla, sugar and yogurt and applesauce, mix well. Add mashed banana to liquid mixture. Pour liquid mixture into dry ingredients and stir until well mixed. Batter should be lumpy. Grease muffin tins with nonstick cooking spray or use paper liners. Fill cups ¾ full. Bake 20 to 25 minutes. Remove from muffin tins when done baking.

Carrie Salisbury   **Monte Vista High School, Spring Valley, CA**

Mile-High Pie

Serves 15-20   **135 Calories, 7 grams fat**

½ cup walnuts, chopped
½ cup shortening or margarine
1 cup flour
¾ cup sugar
1 (10 ounce) package frozen strawberries
2 egg whites
1 tablespoon lemon juice
1 cup cream, whipped

Preheat oven to 350 degrees. Mix together nuts, margarine, flour and ¼ cup sugar and pat into a 9" x 13" pan. Bake 15 minutes. Cool and crumble; set aside. In large bowl, combine strawberries, egg whites, ½ cup sugar and lemon juice. Beat at high speed 20 minutes. Fold in whipped cream. Put ½ crumb mixture in bottom of square or round pan. Pour in filling and top with remaining crumb mixture. Freeze before cutting into squares.

"Light and refreshing dessert on a summer day."

Monica Blanchette   **Landmark Middle School, Moreno Valley, CA**

Orange Biscotti

Makes 40 cookies   **55 Calories, .4 grams fat**

- 2 large eggs
- 2 large egg whites
- 1 cup sugar
- 1 tablespoon orange juice concentrate
- 1 tablespoon orange zest
- 1 teaspoon orange extract
- 2 ¼ cups unbleached all-purpose flour
- 1 teaspoon baking powder
- ½ teaspoon baking soda
- ¼ teaspoon salt
- 1 cup dried apricots or sun-dried cranberries, finely chopped

Preheat oven to 325 degrees. Coat a baking sheet with nonstick cooking spray. Beat the eggs, egg whites, sugar, orange juice concentrate, zest and extract with an electric mixer until smooth. Stir in dry ingredients and fruit. The dough will be sticky, but if it seems too sticky, add a few tablespoons of flour. Spoon dough into 2 logs lengthwise on cookie sheet. Shape with floured hands, leaving ample room for spreading between the rolls and at end of baking sheet. Each roll will spread to about 5" wide during baking. Bake rolls for 20 to 25 minutes, or until lightly browned and slightly firm to the touch. Remove from oven and reduce heat to 300 degrees. Cool baked rolls on baking sheet for 10 minutes. Using a serrated knife, cut each roll into 20 slices. Turn each slice on it's side as it's cut. Bake biscotti for 10 minutes. Turn slices over and bake 10 to 20 minutes more. The biscotti on the ends will be done after 20 minutes total, but the remaining slices may take the full 30 minutes. Cool on wire racks.

"I've left out the orange extract with good results. These go well with espresso."

Myrna Swearingen   **Corona High School, Corona, CA**

Peach Tart

Serves 12   **149 Calories, 6 grams fat**

Pastry:
- 1 cup all-purpose flour
- ¼ teaspoon salt
- ¼ cup margarine, chilled
- 2 to 4 tablespoons cold water

Filling:
- ½ (8 ounce) package reduced calorie cream cheese, softened
- 2 tablespoons sugar

½ teaspoon vanilla
4 or 5 medium peaches or nectarines, peeled, pitted and sliced
½ cup low calorie apple jelly

Preheat oven to 450 degrees. Pastry: In a mixing bowl, combine flour and salt. Cut in chilled margarine until pieces are the size of small peas. Sprinkle 1 tablespoon cold water over part of the mixture. Toss with fork. Push to the side of the bowl. Repeat until all mixture is moistened; form into ball. On a lightly floured surface, roll pastry into a 12" circle. Wrap pastry around the rolling pin. Ease into an 11" flan pan. Do not stretch. Press pastry ½" up sides of the pan. If necessary, trim pastry even with top of pan. Prick bottom of crust well with tines of a fork. Bake 10 to 12 minutes, or until golden. Cool on wire rack. Filling: In small bowl, stir together cream cheese, sugar and vanilla until smooth. Spread atop cooled crust. Arrange peach slices in circles atop cheese mixture. In small saucepan, heat apple jelly until melted. Spoon over peaches. Chill at least 2 hours.

Kris Mehan   **Oroville High School, Oroville, CA**

Pecan Kisses

Makes 3 ½ dozen   **51 Calories, 3 grams fat**
   2 egg whites
   ⅛ teaspoon salt
   2 cups powdered sugar, sifted
   1 teaspoon vinegar
   1 teaspoon vanilla
   1 ½ cups pecan halves

Preheat oven to 300 degrees. In a mixing bowl, beat egg whites with salt until soft peaks form; gradually beat in sugar, vinegar and vanilla and continue beating until very stiff. Fold in pecan halves. Drop by teaspoonfuls onto greased baking sheet. Bake 15 to 20 minutes, or until firm.

Beth Kolberg-Bentle   **Rancho High School, N. Las Vegas, NV**

Raspberry Kisses

Makes 5 dozen   **24 Calories, .4 grams fat**
   1 (3 ounce) package raspberry jello
   1 cup sugar
   ¼ teaspoon salt
   ⅔ cup egg whites (from 5 to 6 eggs)
   ¾ teaspoon almond extract
   1 cup coconut, shredded (optional)

Preheat oven to 250 degrees. Mix together jello, sugar and salt; set aside. Beat egg whites until foamy. Gradually add jello mixture and beat until stiff peaks form. Beat in almond extract. Fold in coconut, if desired. Drop by rounded teaspoonfuls onto brown paper lined baking sheets. Bake 35 minutes.

"Airy and sweet, this is a fun treat. Use any flavor jello you like."

Dale Sheehan   **Santana High School, Santee, CA**

Raspberry Supreme

Serves 10 - 12   **402 Calories, .2 grams fat**

    1 large angelfood cake
    1 large package raspberry jello
    2 cups boiling water
    1 (16 ounce) package Cool Whip
    2 packages frozen raspberries, thawed and drained (reserve juice)
    2 tablespoons cornstarch

Tear angelfood cake into bite-sized pieces and put into a 9" x 13" pan. Dissolve jello in boiling water; let cool slightly. Fold in Cool Whip; add drained raspberries. Pour over cake pieces. Chill until firm. Before serving, in a small saucepan, combine raspberry juice with enough water to make 1 cup. Add cornstarch and cook until clear and bubbly. Cool slightly. Spread glaze over cake and chill until ready to serve.

"This is a recipe from my mother. It can be easily adapted to other fruits. Use sugar free jello and nonfat topping to have a great guilt-free dessert!"

Pam Bonilla   **Valley View High School, Moreno Valley, CA**

Strawberry & Pineapple Delight a la Donna

Serves 9 - 12   **217 Calories, 5 grams fat**

    3 small packages strawberry jello
    2 cups boiling water
    2 (10 ounce) packages frozen strawberries
    1 (3 ounce) can crushed pineapple
    1 (8 ounce) carton sour cream
    Garnish: mint leaves

Dissolve jello in boiling water. Add strawberries and pineapple (makes 7 cups liquid). Pour 3 ½ cups of the liquid into an 8" x 8" glass pan; let set. Spread sour cream over set mixture. Pour remaining 3 ½ cups liquid over sour cream. Let it set up before cutting into squares. Garnish with mint leaves before serving.

"Refreshing addition to a summer barbecue or a festive holiday table
- beats the traditional green jello salad!"

Janet Policy   **Ramona High School, Riverside, CA**

The Edible Fruit Cake

Serves 16   **234 Calories, 4 grams fat**

    3 cups flour
    4 teaspoons baking powder
    ¼ teaspoon salt
    1 teaspoon cinnamon
    ½ teaspoon allspice
    ⅛ teaspoon cloves
    ¼ teaspoon ginger
    1 ⅔ cups sugar
    2 eggs
    2 egg whites
    ¼ cup shortening
    2 tablespoons fruit purée or fat substitute
    1 cup applesauce
    ¼ cup molasses
    1 ½ cups raisins
    1 cup dates, chopped
    ½ cup dried pineapple, chopped

Preheat oven to 350 degrees. Combine flour, baking powder, sugar, salt and spices; set aside. Cream sugar, eggs, egg whites, shortening and fruit purée or fat substitute until light and fluffy. Add applesauce and molasses; mix well. Stir in flour mixture until moist. Gradually fold in fruit. Spread evenly into an angelfood cake pan. Bake 1 hour, or until toothpick inserted in center comes out clean. Invert pan; cool completely. Loosen and remove from pan.

"If you enjoy dried fruit, this is a delightful treat. It is adapted from an old family recipe and revised to be healthier than the original version."

Dale Sheehan   **Santana High School, Santee, CA**

Tropical Blueberry Smoothie

Serves 3   **139 Calories, 2 grams fat**

    1 (8 ounce) can DOLE Crushed Pineapple, drained
    1 ripe DOLE Banana, sliced
    1 cup milk
    1 cup fresh or frozen blueberries

Combine pineapple, banana, milk and blueberries in blender or food processor container. Cover; blend until thick and smooth. Serve immediately. Garnish with banana, strawberry, mint kabob, if desired.

Dole Foods   **San Francisco, CA**

Contributor Index

C

D

E

I

J

K

L

R

S

W

Recipe Index

Frozen Treats

Fruits, Cobblers & Gelatins

Pies and Pastries

Pudding and Custards

Quick Breads

Lighter Desserts

Sweet Surprises

CALIFORNIA
Cookbook

1907 Skycrest Drive, Fullerton, CA 92831

Please send me ____ copy(ies) of *Sweet Surprises* at **$9.95** each (includes tax and postage).

Make checks payable to *California Cookbook Company*.
Enclosed is my check for $_____

Name _____

Street _____

City _____ State _____ Zip _____

Sweet Surprises

CALIFORNIA
Cookbook

1907 Skycrest Drive, Fullerton, CA 92831

Please send me ____ copy(ies) of *Sweet Surprises* at **$9.95** each (includes tax and postage).

Make checks payable to *California Cookbook Company*.
Enclosed is my check for $_____

Name _____

Street _____

City _____ State _____ Zip _____

Sweet Surprises

CALIFORNIA
Cookbook

1907 Skycrest Drive, Fullerton, CA 92831

Please send me ____ copy(ies) of *Sweet Surprises* at **$9.95** each (includes tax and postage).

Make checks payable to *California Cookbook Company*.
Enclosed is my check for $_____

Name _____

Street _____

City _____ State _____ Zip _____